TRUE COACHING

EFFECTIVE COMMUNICATION WITH PARENTS AND ATHLETES

BY TOM DOYLE

with Personal Perceptions Northwest

SAN JUAN PUBLISHING
P.O. Box 923
Woodinville, WA 98072
425-485-2813
sanjuanbooks@yahoo.com
www.sanjuanbooks.com

© 2006 by Tom Doyle

Publisher: Michael D. McCloskey
Design and production: Jennifer Shontz
Editor: Sherrill Carlson

ISBN 0-9707399-6-6
(ISBN-13: 978-0-9707399-6-4)

First Printing 2006
10 9 8 7 6 5 4 3 2 1
Printed in United States of America

ACKNOWLEDGMENTS

Putting together a book like this has been quite an experience. A lifetime of thoughts, experiences, and memories flooded over me as I moved out of 30 years of coaching, teaching, and athletic administration. As I discovered both True Colors and my own true colors, I felt compelled to put pen to paper and attempt to share my thoughts with others.

I am grateful for so many who have made this possible—some by active participation in the writing process, some by walking beside me throughout the years.

I am grateful to those who introduced me to True Colors. Cliff Gillies introduced me to True Colors a number of years ago, then asked me to be involved with developing it in the Pacific Northwest. He was a thoughtful, visionary who believes that True Colors can help make us all better people and help us to deal more effectively with the young people in our schools. Thanks, too, to Ann Kashiwa, another True Colors author (*Meaningful Conversations*), for her encouragement, suggestions, and proofing.

Don Lowry in my mind is a genius. He developed such a simple, yet profound concept. Having used the Myers-Briggs materials for years in schools, I was amazed with how awesome Don's True Colors "tool" is. It is easily understandable by young and old. I am fascinated when presenting True Colors to see the "light bulbs" turn on in participants and to hear the "ah-ha's" cascading from their mouths. Thank you, Don, for such a practical, easy to use and to remember program.

Thanks to all the members of Personal Perceptions Northwest: Joe Richer, Steve Bridge, Don Gillies, and Norm Klug for their input, support, additions, and their playfulness as we went through the process and developed these materials.

Thanks, finally, to Mike McCloskey who believed in me and encouraged and supported the publication and distribution of my materials. They, like me, believe that our kids need a re-commitment on the part of coaches, administrators, and parents to improve the athletic experience. We all hope that this book contributes to that worthwhile goal.

TABLE OF CONTENTS

CHAPTER 1

INTRODUCTION

Congratulations, Coach! You have demonstrated your belief that learning is a life-long process by picking up this book. Your willingness to open yourself to a new, challenging experience could have a dramatic effect on your coaching style, enjoyment, longevity, and effectiveness. Your athletes will benefit as a result of your commitment to excellence. Sit back, relax, and enjoy the exciting information before you.

"They will **Care** how much you **Know**,
when they **Know** how much you **Care**!"

Do you know why kids play sports? The Institute for Studies of Youth Sports at Michigan State University conducted a 1989 study of over 25,000 kids in non school sports and discovered the following dramatic information:

Boys' reasons for participating, ranked according to importance were:

1. To have fun.
2. To do something I am good at.
3. To improve my skills.
4. For the excitement of competition.
5. To stay in shape.
6. For the challenge of competition.
7. To get exercise.
8. To learn new skills.
9. To play as part of a team.
10. To go to a higher level of competition.

Girls' top reasons were:

1. To have fun.
2. To stay in shape.
3. To get exercise.
4. To improve my skill.
5. To do something I am good at.
6. To learn new skills.
7. For the excitement of competition.
8. To play as part of a team.
9. To make new friends.
10. For the challenge of competition.

While an argument can certainly be made that the order of some of these could be altered if the study's clientele had been high school sports athletes, one finds it difficult to argue with the results. Kids play sports to have fun! Competition makes the top-ten list, but demonstrably is a ways down the list.

If the same study were done with coaches, where do you imagine competition and fun would be on that list? High School Coaches have a few competitive bones in their bodies! Coaches can be more preoccupied with preparing teams for competition and for the chance to win than they are in providing an opportunity for fun. Many coaches believe kids can have fun playing pick-up games or intramurals, but that those who choose competitive sports teams do so because they, too, want to experience the success related to putting together a winning team. This is true to a point, but kids won't keep putting in the hard work and long hours if there isn't some fun attached to the commitment.

Now return, if you will, to the statement above… "They will **Care** how much you **Know**, when they **Know** how much you **Care**!" Kids don't really concern themselves with how much you know, with how well you can demonstrate knowledge of an offense or defense or of a particular skill in a particular sport. They do want to know that you care about them. If you demonstrate that and they believe it, they will run or swim through walls for you and think it is "fun."

There are an awful lot of successful coaches out there who use all sorts of differing techniques to reach kids. It is safe to say, though, that the most successful coaches know how to reach kids, to get them to commit to excellence, and usually, this is a result of demonstrating to athletes that the coach likes them, respects them, and is committed to their success. The days of the coach using fear tactics and intimidation to secure the loyalty and commitment of athletes have gone by the wayside.

So how do we get our athletes to understand that we care about them? People of all ages respond favorably to those who care about the person, not just the activity or business in question. Coaches who care get to know their athletes as persons, understand what motivates them, what kind of rewards and feedback is most appreciated, and how to teach and discipline in a manner which is sensitive to the needs of the athletes. They, in turn, will be blessed with athletes who will exceed all expectations.

Coaches need to understand how to effectively communicate with their athletes and their parents. They need to know why kids are participating in their program and what they want out of it. Effective coaches instinctively know that they must adjust their teaching techniques, their strategy, and their style of play with the changing population of kids. They must also be aware of what is immutable in their philosophy and program and be a great salesperson for those critical aspects of their programs.

True Colors will give you an edge in dealing with your teams. It will enhance your ability to communicate with and understand the motivation of your athletes. It will provide opportunity for insight into dealing with problems that may arise with your players or their parents. It will enhance your ability to turn "lemons into lemonade" by providing positive, effective suggestions for being better able to demonstrate clearly to others that you care about them. All of this can be accomplished without making wholesale changes to your existing program, but rather with making subtle changes in your awareness of why people act the way they do and learning how to channel that action in a more positive, focused manner.

Enjoy the journey into True Colors. Try it. Use it. It will change the way you view others and the world in a way that will surprise you. You will wish, like me, that you had heard of this many years ago. I would have made many fewer mistakes along the way. Have fun! Learn to "Brighten your Colors" or to "Fade a Shade" as needed and learn how to help others do the same.

Be a great coach. Let them know how much you care, then they will care how much you know. Then you can achieve so much more than you ever dreamed.

CHAPTER 2

A BRIEF HISTORY AND A COMMON THREAD

The study of human behavior is as old as the human race itself. Early humans must have wondered why others acted the way they did. Recognizing that each person is different and unique certainly led to questions about "why." In 460 B.C. Hippocrates, a Greek physician and philosopher, used four categories to describe common traits in people: Choleric, Melancholic, Sanguine, and Phlegmatic. Another Greek philosopher, Plato, also used four types: Artisans, Guardians, Philosophers, and Scientists.

The famous psychologist, Carl Jung, presented in his 1921 book, *Psychological Type,* four functions of personality: Feeling, Thinking, Sensation, and Intuition. Katherine C. Briggs, and her daughter, Isabel Briggs-Myers included Carl Jung's theories in their work and developed the *Myers-Briggs Type Indicator.* The *Myers-Briggs Type Indicator* breaks down four personality types into sixteen subtypes. The *Myers-Briggs Type Indicator,* a valuable tool in understanding human behavior and matching the workforce to the work, is utilized the world over by business, counseling, education and career professionals.

Coming full circle, David Keirsey and Marilyn Bates published the well-known book *Please Understand Me* in 1967. Their work again identifies four personality types (Apollonian, Promethean, Epimethean and Dionysian). This scholarly program became the basis for the work of Don Lowry, founder of "True Colors."

Don Lowry noted that the complicated structure of previous personality typing theories could be a roadblock to understanding their beneficial practical applications. This inspired him to develop a method anyone can understand and use in their daily lives and careers. Based on David Keirsey's work, Don utilized colors (Blue, Green, Gold and Orange) to develop a metaphor by which people, through self-evaluation, can understand themselves and others more clearly and, as a result, be able to communicate more effectively, especially with those least like them.

True Colors, since 1978, has been taught to thousands of people throughout the world. Don Lowry developed True Colors through his theory of "edutainment" because he believed that communication was most effectively taught through entertainment. In the experience of having fun and being creative, one is most open to new ideas and new awareness.

True Colors provides a great "tool" for our communication toolboxes as we build relationships in our families, with our friends, and at our place of business. The True Colors tools are easily remembered and easily used to enhance the lives of all around us.

CHAPTER 3

WHAT IS TRUE COLORS?

In answering questions, one has to often start out with the negative. So we begin with thoughts about what True Colors is not. True Colors is not an attempt to "pigeon hole" people, to label them, to place them in a particular box, or to find weaknesses in their individual style of doing things. True Colors is not an opportunity for counseling or analyzing individuals. It is not designed to stereotype people into particular categories or ways of behavior.

Very simply, True Colors is a tool, a nonjudgmental language base that enables us to communicate more freely and to appreciate the uniqueness in everyone. True Colors provides understanding that allows us to continue the process of life-long learning as we learn more about ourselves, how we go about our daily work or school lives, and how we relate with those in our lives, our family, our friends, our peers, our student-athletes, our co-workers. True Colors makes it possible for us to better understand how others attempt to communicate with us as well.

One might ask whether the Myers-Briggs Personality Test, which many have taken, doesn't perform the same function. Don Lowry created True Colors in the early '70s because he felt that Myers-Briggs didn't satisfy the needs of many people. Our own personal research indicates that most people who have taken the Myers-Briggs test cannot remember accurately their four letters (e.g. INTJ) test results. Of those who can remember the four letters, few are able to explain what the four letters stand for and how they interact with the others of the sixteen possible results. In other words, the Myers-Briggs test is an excellent and useful tool for those who have grasped and retained its purpose and meaning. But for the average person, it is a fun test to take, interesting to initially get the results, and easily forgotten because it is little used in our daily experience.

True Colors, on the other hand, is a simple, easily understood tool that young and old can use on a daily basis to improve communication with others, especially those who are least like them.

CHAPTER 4

HOW DO WE LEARN?

Academicians have studied the learning process for centuries. Many different paradigms have been developed to help one to understand how learning takes place. It is critical, though, to make the process conscious so that it all makes sense.

In this case, we choose to use the following paradigm for the learning process:

Context

Experience

Reflection

Action

Evaluation

- ◆ *Context*. All learning begins with an attempt to understand the **context** of the learner. We need to understand what the learner brings to the process; we need to meet the learners where they are today. We need to know what the learner "brings to the table" in order for me to coach or teach them well. We need to clearly understand what the learners' experiences of the world are and what the learners' life experiences are. The effect of the school and home environment as well as the way each individual learns help determine how to interact most effectively with our students and athletes.
- ◆ *Experience*. In order to engage the whole person in learning, we need to provide **experiences** that allow them to collect and distill

what they bring to the matter at hand. We will want to guide students in assimilating new information and further experience so they can grow in completeness and truth. To experience something for philosophers meant to "taste something internally" (Ignatius). Coaches are challenged to stimulate students' imagination and the use of senses precisely so that students can enter the reality studied more fully. So, we then use the term, experience, to indicate an activity that considers the cognitive grasp of a subject, but also the inclusion of a sensation of an affective nature registered by the student-athlete.

◆ *Reflection*. The next step in the learning model is **reflection**. How do we help our athletes to be more reflective so that they more deeply understand the significance of what they have learned? In this stage, the learner assimilates facts, tests hypotheses, develops predictions, explores implications, makes explicit what is assumed, achieves personal insights or "ah-ha's," and locates the source of feelings and reactions.

◆ *Action*. Reflection without choosing to do something with this new information can be a wasted moment. So we want next to move our athletes to **action**. Action can be either interior choices, making the truth one's own and remaining open to where that might lead one, or externally manifested choices which impel one to act consistent with the new conviction. Reflection demonstrates maturity when it fosters decision and commitment.

◆ *Evaluation*. The "final" step in the process is **evaluation**. This is an opportunity to assess the growth and learning related to the experiences the athlete is going through. It measures attitudes, actions, and progress on the journey and provides an opportunity for feedback from the coach, diagnostic analysis, goal setting, and a recommitment to the process.

The word "final" has to be used carefully in this context, because the learning process is never completed. Rather than a linear process where the athlete moves from context to experience to reflection to action to evaluation, the motion is seen here more as a spiral than a straight line. There is a constant interaction between the moments of learning. The learner uses the new information gathered to continue to recreate the steps in the paradigm with new information.

TRUE COLORS AND THE LEARNING PARADIGM

The teaching of True Colors grows out of just such a learning paradigm. Nothing happens in a vacuum. There is a pattern of growth that must be appreciated and made conscious. So it is with True Colors that we start with the learners and try to understand what makes them "tick," what perceptions and attitudes they bring to the process of communication, and what their openness is for change and growth.

CONTEXT

We all "tick" differently! What makes one person excited and motivated doesn't move another to action. Some people cry at sad movies, others think they are so sappy that they are humorous. Some people keep their personal spaces neat and clean, others don't waste their time putting things away somewhere. Some are never late for anything, some just can't seem to get anywhere on time. Some work hard all the time, some only at practice, and some only in competition. Some people laugh freely, others seem very reticent to appear to be having a good time. Why is that?

Do you ever try to figure out why you do things the way you do and others don't? Or do you just presume that the others just don't have a clue as to how things ought to be done correctly?

Have you ever heard the comment that "perception is reality?" We seem to understand that others may have different perceptions than we do, but we often can't understand why they don't "get it" and see that their perceptions are wrong. Doesn't everyone think like we do? If they don't, why don't they? Don't they understand they are wrong?

The first step to changing our thinking is to understand. Take a look at the picture of the woman on the next page. Do you see a young woman or an old woman? Can you see both? Which do you see when you look away and come back to the picture? Isn't it interesting that we can all look at the same picture and yet see different things?

Our perceptions of things are normally set in the first 7-30 seconds of our

first interaction with another, or in this case with a picture. We then spend most of the rest of our time defending and justifying our first impression. Only an important, emotional experience can readily change our first impression. So when you see the old lady first, if you come back to this same picture in a month, you will see the old lady first again. You will have to convince your-self the young lady is present and search to find her. The one you saw first will jump out at you. Are we that way with those with whom we come into contact as teachers and coaches, too? Do we form first impressions of our athletes and then find ourselves surprised at a later time? Surprised because the athlete did something we didn't expect or because the athlete never does anything except what we first expected? Maybe it is our perception that creates the surprise. Do the athletes live up to our expectations for them?

Count the number of "F"s in the following sentence. Then close the book for a minute. How many do you come up with?

FINISHED FILES ARE THE RE-
SULT OF YEARS OF SCIENTIF-
IC STUDY COMBINED WITH THE
EXPERIENCE OF MANY YEARS.

What number did you come up with in your count? Be honest! Did you see three? Four? Five? Six? If shown to a group of people, most will say three, a few will see four, a few five, and a smaller number will see six. In fact, there are six. The "F" in the word "of" is commonly left out of the count. First of all, it sounds like a "v", not an "f" and, secondly, we were taught to read right through the little words when we learned to read. So it is easy to understand why most people think there are three "f"s. How is it that we all see the same sentence, words, and letters, yet we answer the question differently? Could it be that our perception may not always be correct and that others may see things differently (and maybe more correctly) than we? Do we sometimes miss the "little things" in our conversations and contacts with others? Horrors!

Remember the sentence with the "F"s anytime you find yourself making judgments about others or about situations. Take a second look. Give it your full attention: Look with your mind and your imagination, not just your eyes! You may be correct, but you may also have made one of those judgments based on erroneous perceptions.

We now know something about our Context, our own situation, about how we communicate and interact with others, which allows us to begin look-ing seriously at how we can learn to communicate more effectively.

EXPERIENCE

True Colors next provides us with an Experience, an opportunity to "taste something internally," to find out more about ourselves and the way we communicate. True Colors believes that conditions ought to be created whereby learners can gather and collect information based on their own experiences and distill that new data to help them become better and more complete communicators.

We begin, then, with the Card Sort. Take out the four character cards accompanying this book. You will see four different colored cards with four sets of mimes involved in various activities and symbols representing different values on each. Lay the four cards out on a table in front of you with the mime and picture side facing up. Do not yet look at the backs of the cards. Looking at the pictures, determine which card is "most like you" and who you perceive yourself to be. Place that card on the left. Select the card that is next "most like you" from the remaining cards and place that next, on the right of the first card. Continue and do the same with the remaining two cards. When finished, you should be able to start on your left with the card "most like you" and proceed to the right to the card "least like you" on the far right.

As an aside, there are three important questions that we need to address. Who do you want to be? Who do you have to be? Who are you? As you look at the cards, try to get in touch with the last question, Who are you?, as that is the critical question.

We all, at times, want to be like someone else or be something we aren't because that is attractive to us. Many high school age students, for instance, want to be Orange because the picture looks like so much fun. They don't want to be Gold because it looks a little boring and it would be difficult to tell their friends that card represents them. So they manipulate the card sort a bit to look like they think they ought to look.

Who do you have to be? Many of us behave differently at work than we might at home. At work, especially as a coach, there is a great need to be organized. You might be very organized there because you have to be, while at home it isn't as important. As parents, we need to be more structured and disciplined sometimes for our kids' sake, so we take on that role. Our friends might even laugh at us when they hear us tell stories about how strict we are at home. They remember when we were the ones causing our own parents grief.

The real question to ponder is, Who are you? Try to follow the directions of the card sort with that in mind. If you do this, you will discover the most accurate portrayal of your Colors and the one that will allow you to understand yourself and others most effectively.

Now, back to the cards. Once satisfied that you have them in the proper order, turn over the cards, read the back, and order them in the same fashion. You may find that the cards stay in the same order or you may find that you need to change the order because of what you read on the back. Keep in mind that not everything on the back may fit you perfectly, but look at the majority of the information as you sort the cards. Some things will just not seem like they fit with you and that is perfectly OK. Order the cards again from left to right from "most like you" to "least like you." Were there any changes in the ordering of the cards? If so, why do you think that occurred?

Next turn to the page titled, "Word Sort." Follow the directions on the page itself. First begin by assigning points under each color. Look again at your cards as they are sorted in front of you. The one on the left, the "most like you," will get the highest point value of 4. Place a 4 on the line under the color that corresponds with the card on your left. Proceed to the next card, the "next most like you" and assign that a 3. Put a 3 on the line below the color that matches your second card. Continue in the same way with the next two cards and the other two colors listed.

Now, reading across the columns, look at the four sets of three words each. For each set of words, place a 4 on the line below the three words that is "most like you", a 3 under the one that is "next most like you", and so on, giving the "least like you" set of words a 1. Do this for each of the five sets of words and lines.

TRUE COLORS WORD SORT

ORANGE	GOLD	BLUE	GREEN

ORANGE	GOLD	BLUE	GREEN
Active	Organized	Nice	Learning
Variety	Plan	Helpful	Science
Sports	Neat	Friends	Privacy
———	———	———	———
Fun	Clean	Caring	Curious
Action	On-Time	People	Ideas
Contests	Honest	Feelings	Questions
———	———	———	———
Playful	Helpful	Kind	Independent
Quick	Trustworthy	Understanding	Exploring
Adventurous	Dependable	Giving	Doing Well
———	———	———	———
Busy	Follow Rules	Sharing	Thinking
Free	Useful	Getting Along	Solving Problems
Winning	Save Money	Animals	Challenge
———	———	———	———
Exciting	Pride	Nature	Books
Lively	Tradition	Easy Going	Math
Hands-On	Do Things Right	Happy Endings	Making Sense
———	———	———	———
Total	Total	Total	Total
ORANGE	GOLD	BLUE	GREEN

SCORE: 4 *the one most like you;* **3** *next most like you;* **2** *the next group;* **1** *least like you.*

When finished, add the numbers down the columns. MAKE SURE TO INCLUDE THE NUMBER UNDER THE COLOR AT THE TOP OF THE PAGE. You should be adding 6 numbers together. The highest total you can come up with in this exercise would be 24. The lowest would be 6. Place the total number on the appropriate line at the bottom of each column. This will later be referred to as your "INTENSITY SCORE."

Order your cards again, using the numbers you just came up with on the "Word Sort." The largest number represents the color of the card that should now be on your left, the one "most like you." Order all the cards using the totaled numbers in the last row. Did your cards change order this time or stay the same? This final ordering of the cards represents your True Colors!

Notice that no one told you what color they thought you ought to be or told you what you are like. You made that determination for yourself. You decided what your own personality temperament was and what your Color order was. It is important to note here that we all have all four colors. We each have our own unique combination of colors that makes us who we are. All Golds are not alike, nor are all Blues, Greens, or Oranges. We tend to act more like our first color at times when we are really stressed, but otherwise, we often move between colors with ease. The combination of our first and second colors gives us a more accurate overall picture of who we are and how we best communicate than the first color alone.

Sorting the cards gave us an experience, an "internal taste," an insight into not only who we are, but how knowing something more about Colors might help us to know and understand those around us better. So where do we go from here?

REFLECTION

The next step in the learning process is to take some time to reflect on what has been learned so that the learner may understand more deeply the significance of what has been learned. One does this by exploring the implications of knowing and understanding the Colors and how they help (or hinder) us in our communications. Now we can begin to make hypotheses and develop predictions about what the Colors mean in our lives as we interface with others.

Let's look at each color individually, then put it all together to see how they might work together.

CATEGORY	BLUE	GOLD
Characteristics	Peacemaker	Prepared
	Optimistic	Loves to plan
	Passionate	Punctual, predictable
	Cause oriented	Responsible
	Cooperative	Values tradition
	Caretaker	Detail oriented
	True romantic	Stable, conservative
Strengths	Communication	Responsible
	Optimism	Detail oriented
	Creativity	Traditional
	Supportiveness	Organization
	Acceptance	Consistent
Stresses	Insincerity	Disloyalty
	Time limits	Change
	Lack of harmony	Lack of control
	Lack of caring	Inconsistency
	Conflict	Ambiguity
Joys	Friendships	Sense of order
	Acceptance	Belonging
	Relationships	Home/Team
	Affection	Time
	Music/Arts	Task satisfaction
Values	Honesty	Loyalty
	Friendship	Dependability
	Sensitivity	Perfection
	Compassion	Responsibility
	Sharing	Honesty

ORANGE	GREEN
Playful	Questions "Why?"
Energetic	Intellectual
Charming	Standard setter
Natural entertainer	Cool, calm, collected
Creative	Perfectionist
Risk taker	Philosophical
Quick witted	"Should be able to"
Confidence	Confidence
Determination	Determination
Mastering tools	Analysis
Getting things done	Technical know-how
Opportunistic	Model development
Time restraints	Too many rules
Unnecessary routine	Incompetence
Waiting	Confusion
Too many rules	Unfairness
Lack of finances	Time deadlines
Being with people	High achievement
Experiencing excitement	Meeting challenges
Performing	Exploring new ideas
Taking risks	Solving problems
Putting plans into action	Seeking new knowledge
Adventure	Intellectual achievement
Fun and play	Logic
Spontaneity	Knowledge
Individual achievement	Competency
Hands-on experience	Technology

It is important to reflect upon a couple of other relevant topics. First, what about introverts and extroverts? Does that make a difference? Of course, whether a person is introverted or extroverted makes a difference in how they are perceived by others in their communications. Introverts tend to gain their energy internally while extroverts find their energy through contact with the world externally. The characteristics are the same, just expressed in a more internal or private way or in an external or public fashion. While this is a somewhat incomplete explanation, especially for the Greens reading it who would like a much more scientific explanation, suffice it to say that much more research needs to be done in this area. It does, however, verify that True Colors is not designed to pigeonhole people, but to provide a language that leads us closer to effective communication.

The second issue is the discussion surrounding "nature" vs. "nurture". There is no pretense here to descriptively define whether one or another is at work here. While we believe that a person is born with certain characteristics designed into their makeup, clearly how one is raised has an effect on our Color makeup. One can change over time as one matures. We sometimes interact with the world with one color at home and another at work. We choose to "brighten" one color over another depending on our role. We do believe, however, that our primary Color remains our primary color in most cases. We do know that when we are stressed, we tend to hold on more tightly to and act out of our primary color.

How can I use True Colors to help me understand others? First, it is critical to note that we tell others what color we are; no one tells us what color we are or what color they think we ought to be. So as we use this tool, we need to be careful to understand that we are taking educated guesses about what color others in our lives are. But we can feel comfortable making those hypotheses so long as we don't try to force others into the color of our expectations.

How about an example? Remember the "Wizard of Oz." See if you can identify the primary colors of each of the main characters:

COLOR

Tin Man	_____
Scarecrow	_____
Lion	_____
Dorothy	_____

What was it that the Tin Man wanted? He wanted a heart; he wanted to feel things deeply. Wouldn't he be an example of a Blue?

Scarecrow clearly was hoping to ask the Wizard to give him a Brain. He, at one point, goes through a very intellectual dialog ending with "E=MC²". Scarecrow perceives himself as a Green.

Lion sees himself as a coward and wants courage. He wants to be noticed and proclaimed the King of the Jungle. He wants to be an Orange.

Dorothy spends much of the story holding the others together with a vision, a vision of a Wizard who can provide for them. She constantly watches out for the others and feels compelled to get them to a place of safety. She focuses throughout the entire movie on trying to figure out how to get home to Kansas and to her family. The Gold values of home and family are prevalent throughout.

Now one could read lots of other ideas into each of the characters and disagree about some of this simplistic analysis, but the characterizations are easily identified.

So how about another example that would allow you to check your skills at recognizing the Colors in others. Look at the next page; see if you can fill in the blanks indicating the possible color of the person driving a car with the following license plates:

TRUE COLORS LICENSE PLATE GAME

Identify which color (or a first and second color) would be most likely to sport the following license plates. Be prepared to explain why you chose those colors:

1. YBNORMAL   _____   _____
2. GRRR8FUL   _____   _____
3. UGOT2BU   _____   _____
4. NTW8N4U   _____   _____
5. TYM2QLT   _____   _____
6. HIONMTS   _____   _____
7. LATE   _____   _____
8. WANDERR   _____   _____
9. CHKMATE   _____   _____
10. TMSCORES   _____   _____
11. N2FISHING   _____   _____
12. PRNCISS   _____   _____
13. IRESCU   _____   _____
14. IX FE   _____   _____
15. 4EN JUNK   _____   _____
16. R U MINE   _____   _____
17. L84AD8   _____   _____
18. LOVMYHON   _____   _____
19. LIV42DA   _____   _____
20. PD2MUCH   _____   _____

Suggest a license plate or two for each of the colors:

GOLD   _____   _____
BLUE   _____   _____
GREEN   _____   _____
ORANGE   _____   _____

What have we learned about ourselves, about our communication, and about others? How might this new understanding help us in our relationships with others?

Hopefully, by now, you have had a number of insights, some "ah-ha's" about yourself. It should now be clear that we all have each of the four colors within us. No one is just one color. We can recognize the Blue, the Orange, the Green, and the Gold in us to varying degrees. We have a primary color that does dominate our spectrum. But, it is the blend of the Colors that makes us truly unique.

By drawing on all of our Colors, we can improve our personal relationships and communication by gaining the knowledge and skills to access the basic core needs of others and of ourselves. Using all of our colors helps us to motivate and empower ourselves and others to use our unique qualities and strengths. This allows us to demonstrate and release our natural talents and skills. Most importantly, it helps us to increase our self-esteem through positive, productive actions.

The hope is that we learn to "Fade a Shade" when our primary color is too strong for the moment. When we realize that our primary color is not allowing us to effectively communicate with and understand someone, we need to choose to "dim" that color and to "brighten" another color. It is in the choosing, the control of our colors, our personality and temperament, that we find growth and develop meaningful relationships with others. We can "choose" to meet others where they are, then try to help them grow along with us by leaning to understand each other.

The key question we asked at the beginning of the section on Reflection was: How can I help my Coaches/Athletes to be more reflective so that they more deeply understand the significance of what they have learned? Communication takes time. Reflection takes time. Coaches, in particular, often do not allow enough time for growth in this area. We are far too concerned with teaching the sport correctly and initiating the technical aspects of a sport. But if we don't allow the time to teach others and to work with others on communicating and understanding each other, the skills and techniques may get lost in the ensuing conflict that arises from "cheating" this critical skill.

ACTION

So now we have considered the context in which we operate, we have had a common experience of the True Colors program, and we have taken time to reflect upon and consider how this can improve our programs. How do we actually go about putting it into action? How can I create an environment where all in my program are positively challenged and changed by what they have learned?

Begin with understanding the language used to communicate with each color. Let's dispel a myth and probably a question on your mind before we start. A coach does not have to coach four different ways nor say things four times so that he can reach kids of each of the colors. But a coach does need to be aware whether the communication form used effectively reaches all the athletes. Salespeople are notorious for knowing their customers so that they know what the needs and values are of the customer before trying to sell them a product. Coaches are trying to sell kids "a product," a system, a means to performance. Wouldn't it also make sense that a coach ought to know the language of each of his "clients," his athletes?

Take into consideration a coach explaining to a linebacker why he needed to fulfill a particular responsibility, to fill a certain hole, in a defensive scheme. If the coach knows True Colors, he can address each, using appropriate motivational language. He might tell the Blue linebacker, "I need you to read the play and fill this particular hole. Your teammates, the defensive end and tackle are responsible for the other two holes here. They will be doing their job, and they need to be able to count on you to do your part to support them. The three of you working together will make this side of the defense impenetrable. Don't let them down." The Blue athlete will be motivated by personal relationships with the others on the defense and will do his best to make all of them look good by doing his job.

The Gold athlete simply needs to be told what his responsibility is. He is task and detail oriented and just wants to know what he is supposed to do. He doesn't want a lot of freedom to choose a course of action, simply tell him what his keys and proper reactions are and he will do the job.

The Green athlete questions "why" on most things. He will want an explanation as to why he has to take that particular hole, because from where he is standing, it appears easier to get to the ball by going a different route. If you explain appropriately why doing it this particular way will put him in the position to make a tackle, he will do as asked and creatively find a way to get the job done.

The Orange linebacker doesn't really want to know the details, he really appreciates being told, "go like a bandit, hit this hole, and make something happen." He will make something happen!

While just saying a coach didn't have to say things in four different ways, we just provided an example that suggested that. But, look more deeply. When dealing with an individual athlete, speak in their language. When speaking to the whole group of linebackers about their responsibility, a coach would incorporate all the points by telling the squad what the expectation of the linebacker is for a particular defensive scheme, what other people on the defense are doing, and how important it is to fulfill their responsibility on the play. A coach touches all the color groups by taking a few more minutes to explain the process and the content of the task.

How do we most effectively work with **Golds**, then?
1. Carry through with what you say you're going to do.
2. Show them the practicality in an idea or an approach.
3. Be on time.
4. Say "thank you" and let them know they are appreciated.
5. Acknowledge them when they do something well.
6. Give them time to plan things.

Coaches should make sure, when working with **Golds**, that they don't:
1. Expect them to be spontaneous.
2. Force them to take risks.
3. Use profane language around them.
4. Demand too much immediate change.
5. Expect them to challenge the established rules.
6. Insist they make decisions without all the facts.

How about working positively with a **Green**, then? Coaches should:

1. Give logical explanations.
2. Allow them time to think about their decisions.
3. Expect them to take a leadership role.
4. Earn their respect.
5. Acknowledge their intelligence.
6. Present data to support ideas.
7. Recognize their need to get to the point quickly.

With **Greens**, don't:

1. Force them to talk about their feelings too much.
2. Become too emotional when arguing with them.
3. Be indecisive.
4. Expect public display of emotions.
5. Take everything they say personally.
5. Embarrass them in public.

When dealing with **Blue** athletes, make sure to:

1. Tell them your personal feelings about any topic.
2. Listen attentively and look at them while talking to them.
3. Tell them what you appreciate about them.
4. Physically touch them (appropriately).
5. Accept their individuality and uniqueness.
6. Allow them to express their feelings.
7. Be honest and sincere.

Be particularly cautious with **Blues**, don't:

1. Be abrupt or cut them off while they are talking.
2. Discount their dreams.
3. Expect them to be confrontational.
4. Compare them to someone else.
5. Deny their emotions or criticize their sensitivity.
6. Ignore them.
7. Take advantage of their kindness.

What about **Orange** athletes? They thrill with feedback and attention, so do:

1. Be upbeat around them.
2. Appreciate their jokes and playful nature.
3. Allow them to be independent.
4. Provide some structure for them, yet be flexible.
5. Respect their need to stay busy doing things.
6. Understand their ability to do several things at the same time.
7. Have fun with them.

And while **Oranges** seem never to be too bothered by much, be careful, and don't:

1. Be intimidated by their energy.
2. Be surprised at their changeable nature.
3. Force them to be too serious about life.
4. Demand that they stick to a strict schedule.
5. Write them off as flakes because of their lightheartedness.
6. Start a "fight" with them unless you intend to fight.

All of this is presented to assist coaches in learning how to best work with their athletes. Coaches can learn to strengthen athletes' perceptions of themselves and, therefore, their self-esteem. Knowing how to effectively motivate athletes using Colors can only enhance both the ability to develop a team and individuals.

It is also important for coaches to understand how others look at them. Remember that we talked about how perceptions can be other's reality? It is critical to know how others might see us so that we can deal with their perceptions and learn to "brighten" or "fade" our colors as needed.

Look at the columns on the next page. Cover the right hand column with your hand for a moment. The left hand column indicates how each Color views itself. The second column lists how others might see a person of that color. These lists can be valuable when working with an individual on improving self-esteem and communication.

How **Golds** See Themselves	How Others May See **Golds**
◆ Firm	◆ Rigid
◆ Conservative	◆ Boring
◆ Strong Willed	◆ Stubborn
◆ Having a View	◆ Opinionated
◆ Orderly	◆ System Bound
◆ Realist	◆ Unimaginative
◆ Stable	◆ Predictable
◆ Directive	◆ Bossy
◆ Moral Standards	◆ Judgmental
◆ Assertive	◆ Controlling

Coaches can work on enhancing the self-esteem of their **Gold** athletes by putting them in situations where tasks and expectations are clearly identified. Give them responsibility for details where that is appropriate. Provide them with opportunities to be of service to others. They enjoy helping in whatever capacity is appropriate in practice and game situations. Give tangible rewards and definitive signs of appreciation for their efforts and accomplishments.

How **Greens** See Themselves	How Others May See **Greens**
◆ Confident	◆ Arrogant
◆ Firm Minded	◆ Merciless
◆ Under Control	◆ Unrealistic
◆ Visionary	◆ Aloof
◆ Calm	◆ Unemotional
◆ Intelligent	◆ Intellectual Snob
◆ Independent	◆ Devalue Relationships
◆ Perfectionist	◆ Critical
◆ Creative	◆ Eccentric
◆ Determined	◆ Heartless

Greens' Self-Esteem can be enhanced by putting them in situations where they are doing things or figuring out how things work. Involve them in some strategy discussions for your sport. Give them challenging tasks that can be accomplished through the use of intellect/knowledge. Give them the opportunity to demonstrate ingenuity by sharing problem solving skills with others on the team. Praise them for their intelligence; encourage them to apply that to relationships.

How **Oranges** See Themselves	How Others May See **Oranges**
◆ Carefree	◆ Flaky
◆ Adventurous	◆ Rule Breaker
◆ Charming	◆ Manipulative
◆ Energetic	◆ Uncontrollable
◆ Bold	◆ Obnoxious
◆ Impulsive	◆ Irresponsible
◆ Flexible	◆ Off Task
◆ Enjoys Process	◆ Resists Closure
◆ Shares Decision Making	◆ Indecisive
◆ Changing	◆ Distracted

The best suggestions for working with **Orange** athletes and their self-esteem are finding ways to include their active participation. Put them in active, hands-on situations during your practice sessions. Give them opportunity to role-play, to trouble-shoot a difficulty or problem. Allow them to demonstrate the skills that you are introducing into the practice session. Provide them an opportunity for leadership in an area of their proficiency. Create situations in which they can be successful. Give them immediate feedback for positive, constructive contributions. If a coach waits till tomorrow to discuss a conflict or a problem with an Orange, the Orange may likely have already put it in the past and moved on, so immediate feedback is important.

How **Blues** See Themselves	How Others May See **Blues**
◆ Compassionate	◆ Bleeding Heart
◆ Trusting	◆ Naïve
◆ Romantic	◆ Mushy
◆ Affectionate	◆ Touchy-feely
◆ Caretaker	◆ Smothering
◆ Nostalgic	◆ Stuck in the Past
◆ Sympathetic	◆ Push-over
◆ Sensitive	◆ Emotional
◆ Nurturing	◆ Fawning
◆ Passionate	◆ Always a Cause

With **Blue** athletes, a coach can enhance their self-esteem by creating situations where they work with other people. Blues don't like working by themselves; they prefer working with another on tasks or skills. Enlist their help in planning activities that will make them feel like they have a real stake and are involved in the process. Provide them with opportunities to nurture others. They are great sources of positive feedback and positive comments for teammates. Encourage that. Give attention and approval when they perform in a manner that contributes to others. Reinforce their behavior that contributes to your team's success.

Putting True Colors into action takes some practice and some effort. Mostly it takes making a constructive, positive choice to pay attention to what motivates and informs the athletes that we have the great opportunity to work with daily. Our actions demonstrate our commitment and our convictions. Actions are the result of a conscious choice to try to communicate more effectively. They are a result of creating an environment that positively challenges and changes everyone on our teams as a result of what they are learning.

EVALUATION

The final step in the learning process (before it begins anew, of course) is Evaluation. Those who are life-long learners constantly reflect on what they are doing, how effective it is, and how they can do it better next time. This is a critical aspect of the learning process, one that, too often, is ignored. So it is with coaches; they need to look at every aspect of their program to determine whether their practice plan has worked, whether they have effectively communicated with their athletes and parents, whether there might be a better way to approach their work. We need to create reflective space to allow this to happen. We need to allow our athletes and parents to provide some feedback as well as asking administrators to assist in our growth.

This is a time for questioning; sometimes we may even be able to answer the questions. Other times, the question itself provides a jumping off point for further discussion and analysis. Questioning involves risk. We may find out that what we have been doing isn't working. That can be a frightening result. If we don't have supportive people around us, it may prevent us from asking the really difficult questions that we need to respond to the most. Have courage. Growth sometimes, most of the time, is accompanied by some pain. We preach to our athletes that we learn more from our failures than from our successes. We must practice what we preach and ask the difficult questions.

See what kind of answers you can come up with for the following questions, then add some of your own:

- What Color is your job?
- What Color is your sport?
- Is there a Color for an athlete that is most suited for your sport?
- How can we teach our athletes to brighten this sport's critical color(s)?
- What Colors are your assistant coaches?
- What Colors are your athletes?
- Am I able to effectively motivate each Color of athlete?
- Am I effectively able to discipline each Color?
- Do I need to change my strategies for teaching skills to reach different Colors?
- What potential conflicts arise out of these Colors?
- What are the benefits to having each of the Colors on your staff?
- What are the benefits of having each of the Colors on your team?
- What is my least Color? Do I communicate effectively with those of my least Color? How do I brighten that Color?
- How do I teach skills? Does knowing about Colors influence me to use different methods for my athletes?

- When stressed by competition, by parent situations, or in dealing with my athletes, does my primary Color dominate?
- Knowing my Color spectrum, how do my athletes know that I care about them?

Please take time to add to the list of questions. Reflecting on the successes and failures of the sport's season is critical to improving a coach's skills and relationships with the athletes.

We all love to win and to demonstrate our successes on the playing surfaces of our particular sport. But it is fascinating to look at the goals and philosophies representing why sports programs exist. The most common reasons for a school, a park department, or an outside agency to start programs are:

- To work with others –The Victory of the WE over the I.
- To be successful - We do not always win, but we succeed when we continually STRIVE to WIN. "Winning is not everything—but making effort to win is!" (Vince Lombardi)
- To develop sportsmanship.
- To improve—skill development strengthens self-image.
- To enjoy athletics.
- To develop desirable personal health habits.

Sports, we believe, are a wonderful way to teach individuals about the importance of sacrificing self for others, the victory of the "We" over the "I." It provides an excellent opportunity to teach the values of hard work and effort—that trying to win is sometimes more critical to our future success than winning itself.

Who does not think that athletics ought to be the place where we teach the lessons of sportsmanship? Former President Bill Clinton, playing recently in a charity event in Florida for tsunami victims, spoke of the "mystical" nature of golf. He discussed it as the only sport that requires an athlete to know the rules and to self-enforce them. Did you ever wonder why that shouldn't apply to all sports? Now we do have officials in most sports, but do we want to teach our athletes that anything an official doesn't call is OK? Don't we want to teach our athletes how to respect their opponents so that, win or lose, they are able to shake hands and thank them for showing respect to us by playing their best?

Isn't athletics created to help athletes develop skills? Skill development may be one of the more critical steps in developing an individual's self-image. When athletes develop a skill and can do something they were not previously able to do, they feel good about themselves. Self-image is not a result of how often someone else tells athletes how good they are, but how often the athletes feel the success of learning something new and demonstrating this new-found ability in their actions.

If we are not teaching athletes how to enjoy themselves and the sport, how long will they continue? Today, more and more often, athletes are quitting sports programs before they ever reach the high school level because of parental pressures or because playing the sport is no longer any fun. We know from our experience and the research that the reason both boys and girls participate in sports programs is to have fun. Competition comes in about 4th in the top ten reasons list for boys and about 6th for girls. If it isn't fun, they will not continue to put in the time, energy, and effort to succeed.

An additional reason for sports programs is to teach athletes the healthy lifetime habits related to exercise and competition. We want our kids to learn to take care of their minds and their bodies as they age. Athletics are a great training ground for what we hope will be life-long habits.

Interestingly, what is not on this list may be more telling than the things that made the list. The things that don't show up on our lists of why we have sports programs are winning league and state championships and earning college scholarships. While these are sometimes by-products of our programs, we do not often hear of those as primary reasons for selling our sports programs to kids and parents.

Our evaluation of our programs needs to include some attention to these other, more difficult to measure, goals. This may be the most critical assessment that we need to attend to in our deliberations.

Ultimately what we want to accomplish in our coaching is to develop a climate that supports everyone's positive attitudes and attributes. In order to do this, we need to "brighten" our Colors and teach others how to do the same. In other cases, we need to learn to "Fade a Shade" if necessary so that we can be more sensitive to the needs of others with whom we are building a relationship. We need to instill in every member of our team a philosophy that emphasizes the "Victory of the 'WE' over the 'I.'" We need to preach the virtue of, and reward the practice of, hard work. And, probably most of all, we need to keep clearly in mind that our athletes will CARE how much we KNOW when they KNOW how much we CARE!

True Colors provides a non-judgmental language base to enable us to communicate more freely and appreciate the uniqueness in everyone. What does that phrase, non-judgmental language base, mean? It means that we can take some of the emotion out of a conversation or conflict through reference to Colors. For example, a Gold parent, who feels that being on time and being responsible are critical attributes of a mature person, is going to be in conflict with a son or daughter who is an Orange and doesn't find being on time or looking forward to tomorrow to be all that important. You can imagine the fights in that household about being late and about the parent being bossy and rigid. If instead of calling each other names (lazy, boring, undisciplined, rigid), the parent can simply say to the child, "You are acting kind of Orange about this," and the child can respond, "You are being kind of Gold in your reaction here," much of the emotion and conflict can be lessened. It is a language that doesn't attach a judgment to a Color; it is simply a statement of fact that then allows an opportunity for both sides to have a laugh, a reminder of their differing motivations, and a chance to meet in the middle somewhere.

Begin, right now, to put True Colors to work to make the athlete's experience of your program the best it can be. Show your True Colors!

CHAPTER 5

TRUE COLORS—CUP OF LIFE

It is such a cliché that we sometimes use it and don't even think about it. But it is critical to understand the relevance of the question, "is the cup half full or half empty?" True Colors helps us to get a clearer picture of the real answer to this question.

After "Coloring up" participants at a True Colors seminar, it is fun to ask the group whether the cup I am holding in my hand is half full or half empty. When asked, most often the Golds answer, "It is half empty." The Blues respond, "It is half full." Often when the Greens are asked, the will respond, "I don't know, I need to measure it to find out." They don't want to commit to an answer unless they can intellectually know they are correct. Oranges will not care which it is; they just want to know if it is drinkable. It is fantastic to listen to one group after another give similar answers.

- ◆ Gold—Golds are realists and see the problems of the world and see the Cup as half empty.
- ◆ Blue—Blues are optimistic and see the wonders of the world and view the Cup as half full.
- ◆ Green—Greens analyze and ponder the "gray" of the world, and would measure the Cup to see which it is.
- ◆ Orange—Oranges love being in the world, in the "here and now," and would just as soon drink the Cup.

Life is a lot more fun when we include all four colors. We need to be realistic when we are trying to solve problems, but we need to be optimistic about the outcome as well. We need people around us who can be analytical and creative in problem solving. And we need people who help us get "it" done when we come to a decision on how to proceed.

How about some other examples to support the need for all colors in our lives!

Several of the people we work with went to a True Colors Advanced Class Training recently and were put into groups by our colors. We were then asked to respond in a sentence or two what we would do if we met a "Bear in the Woods." It was fascinating to see how each color responded. The Greens reported that they would analyze the situation, deciding if there were a cub or food in the area, which would make the bear more dangerous. After the analysis, they would decide a course of action. The Blues in their group indicated their first reaction was how cute the bear was; then they started praying because they knew they were in trouble; then they felt badly because they realized they had invaded the bear's territory and it was their fault if anything happened. The Oranges described how "cool" it was to be in the woods and so close to a real bear in the woods. When they realized they were in trouble, their first thought was that they only needed to outrun one other person there to be safe. The Golds reported that they wouldn't even have gone into the woods without a gun or pepper spray.

How differently we look at the world. How important it is that we have all four colors in our lives. How creative can we be if we learn to use all four colors to solve problems and to create new opportunities in our families, our schools, and our jobs?

I jokingly tell the story in seminars of the differences in the colors as we drive down the "freeway of life." Golds get in their cars, determine the speed limit (let's presume it is 60 mph) and drive either at or just above that. They probably set their cruise control next. They know right and wrong, know the limits, and they go on with their lives.

As they drive down the road, a car driven by a Green passes them. The Green has determined that the freeway was designed for at least 75 mph and the car was manufactured with much higher speeds in mind. The Green is confident about the locations of the potential speed traps and is willing to exceed the 60 mph limit. Greens have creative ideas and things to do. They have to keep moving.

The Orange may not even know there is a speedometer in the car or if the Oranges know that, they may not pay much attention to it. They like speed and pushing limits, they may be late, and they may exceed the limit as well. The Oranges live life to the fullest and can't afford to waste time getting where they are going.

The Blues often exceed the limits because they are so passionately involved in a conversation that they don't even know they are exceeding the limit. In fact, it won't be long before they come back to the cruise control Gold because they are talking to the person in the front seat or someone on a cell phone. They may drive 70 mph for a while, then 50 mph. They get focused on what is important to them and give 100% to that person or event.

All the colors find their joys and needs fulfilled by following their True Color. One view of the world is not better than another or worse than another. They are just different ways of viewing our lives. How rich those lives can be if we can enrich it with a kaleidoscope of Color!

The obvious point of all this is that it ought to be clear that we need all four types, all four colors. True Colors gives us the opportunity for insight into how to get the most out of life. Whether we "brighten" our own colors or surround ourselves with people of other colors matters little. What does matter is that life is best lived in COLOR.

CHAPTER 6

RELATING TO THE
ACTIVE ORANGE ATHLETE

CORE NEED & VALUE:

◆ Sense of Freedom

ATTRIBUTES:

◆ Playful
◆ Energetic
◆ Charming
◆ Natural entertainer
◆ Master negotiator
◆ Tests limits
◆ Quick witted
◆ Creative, inventive
◆ Likes tangible rewards
◆ Risk taker
◆ Visual, kinesthetic
◆ Pushes the boundaries
◆ Natural non-conformist
◆ Thrives on competition
◆ Focused on externals
◆ Appreciates immediate feedback
◆ Impulsive, spontaneous
◆ "Just do it"
◆ Most productive in informal environments

Orange athletes thrive in competitive practices. They enjoy practices that have variety in drills and that are fun. They are concerned with a high level of skill and maximum success. They like to see direct results by the end of practice. Orange athletes find that routine and day after day "sameness" in a practice can be a challenge. It is not their top priority! They believe in the value of team unity. Orange athletes can be very demanding and need to know the coach is concerned about their success.

Orange athletes have a tough time with long meetings. They are active and enjoy hands on activities. Meetings that are short and to the point are best for Oranges. When in conflict with an Orange Athlete, be direct, but not confrontational. They may see conflict as a competition and respond with an "I am going to win" attitude.

Orange athletes are "gamers." They love competition and normally put on a "game face" and excel during competition. Orange athletes are far more focused at game time than they are in a practice setting. The trick with Orange athletes is to get them to practice with enthusiasm as they find this far less exciting than actual competitions.

Coaches need to understand these athletes. They can often be labeled as "troublemakers" because they seem unfocused. When coaches realize that Orange athletes love hands-on opportunities and dislike standing around or standing in lines, it might help explain why Orange athletes more frequently than others get involved in horse-play at practice. Knowing this can help a coach design more effective practice plans to keep the interest of the Orange athletes.

Orange athletes thrive on freedom, variety, recognition, and action and activity. Keep practices exciting by providing a wide variety of activities and drills. Change drills frequently. Allow Orange athletes some freedom to be creative in their reactions within drills and in their performances. Orange athletes need immediate feedback on their actions. If a coach waits till after practice or until the next day to provide input for Oranges, the athlete likely will not even remember the situation the coach makes reference to, as the Orange athlete lives in the moment and has already moved on.

Orange athletes yearn to be recognized for their quick-witted sense of humor and ideas. They appreciate tangible rewards for their accomplishments. In a sport like football, for instance, Oranges would love the helmet decals given out for special things like fumble recoveries, interceptions, great blocks, or the like.

These athletes thrive on adventure and fun. They are very spontaneous, must have hands-on opportunities to learn their sport, and get a personal thrill out of their own individual achievement. The coach needs to learn to help these athletes focus on the larger picture and on the team concept of the sport.

Being with teammates brings the Orange athlete great joy. They love the interaction between friends and teammates, especially when it is intermixed with some fun and "wisecracking." They love to take risks and find that playing in a competitive contest is the highlight of their day.

Oranges are confident in their abilities, even if that confidence is not yet deserved. They have a great sense of determination in a competitive situation and hate to lose. They have great instincts and find ways to get things done that others may not have the energy for or even see as possibilities.

Time stresses Orange athletes if there are strict timelines that must be met. They tend to accomplish things at their own pace, often distracted by other things or people as they process, but they will get them done given enough time. Routine, especially unnecessary routine, drives the Orange athlete crazy. They hate standing in line because they "just want to do it" rather than watching others. While they also are stressed by too many rules, and any rules can be too many, they will comply so long as there are frequent reminders and feedback during the process.

PRACTICE ENVIRONMENT

Coaching athletes would be simple if all responded to the same stimulus in the same fashion. Obviously, that is not the case, so coaches need to reach back, reflect on the needs of the "Colors," and create an environment that is appropriate for the athletes on that team.

Orange athletes thrive in a less structured, free wheeling practice regimen that is filled with exciting, challenging, competitive drills and activities. They desperately want there to be some fun, or they will find a way to create some. The coach may not appreciate their definition of fun in the middle of a practice plan, so ought to prepare for it by making sure there is an element of fun in the session. Within reason, be playful with Orange athletes, but be sure to maintain your distance as they might interpret it as an invitation to act that way all the time. Orange athletes are very spontaneous and love when the coach comes up with a drill that demonstrates their athletic prowess or gives them a chance to demonstrate a set of skills for the rest of the team. Create practices and drills that allow for competition and game-like situations.

ENHANCING SELF ESTEEM IN THE ORANGE ATHLETE

Orange athletes' esteem is enhanced when they feel the coach gives them some flexibility in their role on the team, when their coach exhibits enthusiasm and optimism for their skills, and when the coach recognizes their value to the team. They love it when they are encouraged to try new skills and techniques, because this is inherent in their personality. They like their coach to offer positive and specific feedback about their performance. Praise from their coaches and teammates about their ability to get things done boosts their self worth immeasurably.

Coaches should encourage Orange athletes to be spontaneous, but open to new ideas. While encouraging competitiveness, coaches need to remind Oranges to be actively involved in those routine, "we just have to do them" drills at practice.

Oranges love recognition and expect honest critiques from their coaches. They don't hold on to criticism for very long, but it is best to provide them with positive and specific feedback on their performance. Provide tangible results for them, work with them to set short term goals, including practice or drill goals, and the coach will have much more success with Oranges. Validate their talent, put them in leadership roles, share your sense of humor with them, and the coach will find that Orange athletes can be very cooperative and positive, contributing members of the squad.

Make sure to explain, directly and clearly, expectations for Oranges. Be aware that they have a dramatic effect on the rest of the team because they are so outspoken and out front at all times. Praise them for their skill, their ability to "get it done," and their creativity.

MOTIVATING SKILL DEVELOPMENT AND SUCCESS

Orange athletes are motivated by a coach who minimizes structure, helps them understand the desired goals, and provides them with the freedom to be creative in reaching those goals. They like using their mental and physical abilities to perform on their team. They are motivated by their coach's acknowledgment of their competence in performing their team role and individual skills. Public "pats on the back" are extremely motivational. Allowing them the freedom to build on what they have learned and to create new ways to accomplish team goals is ideal.

Coaches can effectively motivate Orange athletes by focusing on the immediate, being clear on what is expected in drill and practice routines, and rewarding achievement quickly. Orange athletes will respond best to the enthusiastic coach who demonstrates spontaneity and humor.

Orange athletes are known for their competitiveness, their leadership, their skill, their social interactivity, and their adventurous nature. Take advantage of these wonderful characteristics as they may provide great modeling for other teammates. Be ready to provide immediate feedback when these characteristics go over the line of what you expect, however.

Bring out the best in Oranges by changing activities frequently, by allowing competitive or one-on-one drills, and allowing them to demonstrate new skills or drills. Reward them for their quickness of action and their very unique contributions to the team. Allow them some time during the session to interact with teammates, while getting water on a break or changing drills, so that their rich sense of humor can come out without distracting others or interrupting your practice.

GAINING ORANGE ATHLETE'S COOPERATION

The Coach gains Orange athletes' cooperation by providing an atmosphere that encourages them to try new ideas and to perform with some freedom. Their coaches should provide them with specific and immediate feedback and assist them in setting short-term goals that are appropriate for the team. Implementation of those goals needs to be flexible and exciting.

Orange athletes love practices that are competitive and drills that require a reasonable amount of chance or risk. They prefer hands-on learning to mental practice. They need someone to help them set short-term goals for a practice session and for the drills at hand. They want to accomplish a skill, and then move onto something new.

Coaches can keep Oranges actively involved in practice by providing feedback and encouragement that tells Oranges they are leaders, that their great enthusiasm is catching, and that they are leaders who have a tremendous influence on their teammates.

Coaches should provide brief, concise instructions, short motivational speeches, and encourage Orange athletes to have patience with themselves and their skill development. Coaches should teach these athletes about both short and long term goals, appeal to their sense of competitiveness, and remind them that being a team player is as important as being the star of the team.

TROUBLESHOOTING PROBLEMS WITH THE ORANGE ATHLETE

Orange Athletes find conflict with their coach when there is not a line of direct, immediate communication. They want the freedom to adjust in midstream and the flexibility to try out new skills and ideas. When they have conflict, remember the age-old adage of "praising in public, criticizing in private." Remember to use some humor and not to back them into a corner as they might react poorly. Provide them with short-term goals, frequent opportunities to get feedback, let them know what they are doing right, and they will react to criticism much better.

When conflict arises with an Orange athlete, coaches need to evaluate themselves to discover whether they have provided enough enthusiasm and activity to keep Oranges interested. Has the coach provided physical opportunities rather than just the mental learning opportunities of a chalk talk? Has the coach provided both the opportunity to learn the skill and strategy of the sport as well as made it entertaining?

Reflection by the coach in conflict with Orange athletes should include: have I acknowledged their contributions and accomplishments; have I helped them to develop both long and short term goals; have I offered them feedback and used positive reinforcement to motivate them; and have I encouraged them to develop positive team behaviors?

Coaches who take a good, hard look at themselves and their reactions to their Orange athletes can go a long way to improving testy relationships by understanding what makes Oranges "tick" and modifying their own responses to their athletes. By remembering that there is usually more than one side to a story or to a problem, coaches can head off conflict by taking a proactive approach to their athletes.

DISCIPLINING ORANGE ATHLETES

When Orange Athletes are disciplined, they prefer immediate feedback that is specific and non-confrontational. They value knowing that their coaches feel they are competent and getting the job done. They appreciate opportunities for growth in a one-on-one environment.

Discipline situations arise with Oranges when they feel trapped, backed into a corner. At times they have difficulty grasping concepts or skills because their competitive nature requires them to be good at it right now. They get frustrated when they don't "get it" right now. Orange athletes tend to resist rules and regulations, so a coach needs to get them involved in setting some of the rules, understanding why those rules exist, and getting immediate feedback when they don't live by these rules. Discipline situations also arise when Oranges don't feel appreciated and when they stand around too long or get bored because they aren't active enough.

When discipline situations come up and coaches need to meet with Orange athletes, they should keep a sense of humor, not react to interruptions or clever remarks by the athlete, keep the meeting private and short, and avoid confrontations. Orange athletes tend to want to compete. If the only competition they can find is verbal sparring with a coach, they may very well choose to get into that competition. The coach should be aware of and recognize this and avoid such a match.

Always end meetings with Oranges by telling them that you expect nothing less than their best effort, remind them of their past successes, let them know that you are on their side and want them to be successful, and shake their hand or pat them on the back.

SOME FINAL THOUGHTS ON ORANGE ATHLETES

Coaches may find it helpful, when dealing with Orange athletes in a one-on-one situation to show them the following charts. This is most effectively done by placing a hand over the second list ("How Others May See Oranges"), and asking the Orange athletes if the first list describes how they see themselves. The answer will undoubtedly be in the positive. Next, uncover the chart of "How Others May See Oranges."

HOW ORANGES SEE THEMSELVES:

1. Carefree
2. Adventurous
3. Charming
4. Energetic
5. Bold
6. Impulsive
7. Flexible
8. Enjoys Process
9. Shares Decision Making
10. Changing

HOW OTHERS MAY SEE ORANGES:

1. Flaky
2. Rule Breaker
3. Manipulative
4. Uncontrollable
5. Obnoxious
6. Irresponsible
7. Off Task
8. Resists Closures
9. Indecisive
10. Distracted

This may be an eye opener for the athlete. This provides a great opportunity for a discussion about "perception" and how "perception sometimes becomes another's reality."

Ask the Orange athletes if they are comfortable with the description of them in the second list. This should provide a great opportunity for coaches and athletes to have a discussion about "where to go from here." Don't be surprised if you get a flippant comment from the Oranges such as, "We don't care which view people have of us." That also gives a great opening for a discussion about caring, of being a teammate, of putting the "WE" before the "I" on your team.

Orange athletes may be the best athletes, the most competitive kids in your program. They are "gamers" who may not be quite as interested in practice as they are in contests. The can disrupt your practices because they are bored or they can provide tremendous leadership if you can creatively keep them involved. They are energetic and playful and can provide some of the fun that all your athletes need to stay involved in your program. Encourage your Orange athletes to be involved, to provide leadership, and to be a positive role model and teammate. They will reward you with fun, excitement, and a fiery, competitive attitude.

CHAPTER 7

RELATING TO THE
INDEPENDENT GREEN ATHLETE

CORE NEED & VALUE:

◆ Sense of Intellectual Competence

ATTRIBUTES:

◆ "Should be able to"
◆ Questions "why"
◆ Visionary, futurist
◆ Can never know enough
◆ Intellectual
◆ Standard setter
◆ Theoretical
◆ Idea person
◆ Cool, calm, collected
◆ Perfectionist
◆ Work is play—play is work
◆ Philosophical
◆ Complex
◆ Often not in the mainstream
◆ Abstract, conceptual, global
◆ Independent
◆ Logical
◆ Explores all facets before deciding

Green athletes find enjoyment in out-playing their opponents. They enjoy team sports because of the strategy involved. Green athletes may question the rules and regulations of the coach because they have a need to understand "why?" If the coach is having a problem with the team, Green athletes enjoy being asked to help find a solution. They expect their teammates to work hard and strive for perfection. They do not show their emotions readily and do not respond well to emotional outbursts.

Green athletes may be a coach's greatest challenge. These athletes are great competitors, but they prefer to work independently and often question "why" things are done the way they are. A coach may see this as a challenge to authority, but often it is simply a matter of the need to know that Green athletes possess. Green athletes may also spend so much time analyzing situations that they can't make the quick decisions sometimes necessary in an athletic competition. Sometimes their focus on perfection leads to setting standards for themselves and others that are not possible to accomplish.

On the positive side, Green athletes are perfectionists who will work to get things right. They analyze situations well, are logical in their approach to new situations, and remain calm in stressful situations. All these characteristics help athletes to perform better. Green athletes also love to be in leadership positions and coaches can count on them to perform to high standards.

Green athletes thrive when coaches give them the opportunity to ask questions and to make suggestions for better ways of doing things. Coaches need to help these athletes find appropriate forums for doing this, but will find they cooperate much more when allowed to be involved. Green athletes need factual and truthful discussions about why decisions are made and why particular rules are necessary. Then they will buy into the program and support it fully.

Green athletes want to be recognized for their ideas and appreciated for their efforts. They expect accuracy and high standards from all around them. They need to be clear on what the requirements are for them.

Green athletes are impressed when their coach demonstrates logic and knowledge in preparation for an opponent. They expect competency from their coach and love it when technology is employed in the practice and contest situations.

Green athletes' strengths include their determination, confidence, and analytical abilities. Count on the Green athletes to work to the best of their abilities because of their desire for perfection. Work with them on realistic expectations, then get out of the way and watch them go. Their confidence in their ability will be infectious and help the team to feel better going into a competitive situation. Coaches can count on their Green athletes to analyze new situations and to be creative in solving problems.

Green athletes will perform below their ability if they feel there are too many rules, they are surrounded by incompetence, they perceive that their coach treats some kids unfairly, or there are strict time guidelines that must be met. Green athletes need time to analyze and consider things. There is a fine line between giving them too little time to really think through a problem and spending too much time as they have already figured out a response and moved on.

PRACTICE ENVIRONMENT

Green athletes work best in a practice environment that allows some opportunity for creativity and independent work on skill development. They enjoy the mental aspect of the game; the chess match part of a contest. They get a great deal out of watching film, using technology, or walking through a situation that might occur in a contest and can translate that into action in competition. They are happy to work on a skill independently until they get it right, and then want to move on to another.

ENHANCING SELF-ESTEEM IN THE GREEN ATHLETE

Green athletes' esteem is enhanced when the coach acknowledges their intelligence. They like to be recognized for their value and the usefulness of their input. Green athletes like it when coaches and athletes appreciate and have an easy-going attitude toward their different approach to thinking, talking, and behaving. Allowing them to work independently at times and to creatively develop their skills is perfect for their personalities.

Coaches can get the most of out their Green athletes by encouraging them to be inquisitive and creative. If coaches can work out practice plans in such a way as to give Green athletes the time and opportunity to offer solutions based on their observations, the Green athletes will reward them with new insights.

Green athletes need positive and very specific feedback on their progress at practices. Coaches who create practice scenarios that challenge these athletes to use their intellects will see them grow. Green athletes should be encouraged to work with others. They prefer to work independently, yet they have a need to be in leadership positions and this provides a great opportunity for them to try out that role.

Coaches should provide precise information to their Green athletes, encourage them in their quest for improvement, and be receptive to their observations and opinions. Praise Green athletes for their competence, creativity, and resourcefulness.

MOTIVATING SKILL DEVELOPMENT AND SUCCESS

As Green athletes, they are motivated when the coach encourages them to use their analytical abilities to creatively perform their roles. The coach can motivate them by allowing them to use their intellectual creativity to reach new solutions to problems. They are motivated by recognition of their skill in "outsmarting" the competition. They like to be encouraged to think, be inquisitive, and explore better ways to do things.

Green athletes are impressed when their coaches are confident and creative. They enjoy the logic of preparation for competing with an opponent. They appreciate it when their coaches provide challenges that test their abilities.

Green athletes find enjoyment in accomplishing tasks that require analysis, competence, and intellectual thought. Coaches can find opportunities to challenge these athletes in practice situations, in contest preparations, and in team building activities.

If a coach can create practice situations that allow the Green athletes to find creative solutions in drills and activities to problems presented, the best learning takes place. One-on-one drills, or drills versus a clock, are excellent opportunities for Green athletes to learn and develop both skills and confidence. Providing "chalk talks" or video experiences also bring out the best in the Green athletes as they can use their intellectual skills in a positive way.

GAINING THE GREEN ATHLETE'S COOPERATION

Green athletes are most cooperative when they feel the coach encourages them to use their intellect and reasoning skills. Green athletes like the fact that their coaches give them problems to solve without a specific time frame. They enjoy other athletes asking them for their opinion, which encourages them to interact more.

Green athletes admire coaches who are objective and logical, concise and analytical. They very much appreciate seeing that their coaches are focused on the task at hand. They will cooperate with a coach who challenges them while encouraging them to improve.

Green athletes require positive feedback on their skills. They would like specific information on how they are doing rather than just an "atta way to go." They thrive on opportunities to demonstrate their competence in drills or activities. They thrill with a chance to evaluate a situation themselves and come up with alternative solutions. They especially appreciate it when their coaches express appreciation for their contributions.

Coaches can help Green athletes by helping them to stay focused on the task at hand. They can sometimes get so caught up in the big picture of things that they miss out on the importance of the little things along the way. Reminding them of the need to focus and to stay on track with short term goals can be particularly helpful to Green athletes.

TROUBLESHOOTING PROBLEMS WITH THE GREEN ATHLETE

Green athletes feel unappreciated when the coach does not acknowledge their abilities to solve problems. They can find a solution to a problem if the coach will allow them to use their ability to analyze the situation. They utilize their skills most effectively when they understand the goals clearly, but can pursue their own means to reach it. Some people feel they are aloof, but they need to know Green Athletes just value their independence and are not emotional. The coaching staff needs to give them some room and time to think.

When faced with problems with Green athletes, coaches can ask themselves if they have allowed those critical characteristics of the Green athletes to come to the forefront. Have they allowed these athletes to use and to demonstrate their creativity and analytical abilities? Have the coaches allowed for individual work by these athletes? Have they created situations at practice that allow for some creativity in the Green athletes' assignments?

Coaches will have fewer problems with Green athletes if they talk with them and share their understanding of the values that are necessary for success in their sport. If the coaches take the time to help the Green athletes understand the need for a particular rule or regulation for team conduct, these athletes will be supportive. If coaches use positive reinforcement and encourage the Green athletes to develop positive team behaviors, they will be great team leaders.

DISCIPLINING THE GREEN ATHLETE

When Green athletes are disciplined, they react favorably when the coach keeps the session focused on their actions and not on their ideas. Green athletes do not appreciate sarcasm and prefer being allowed to explain their position. Being reminded of their special talents can diffuse the situation.

Discipline situations arise with Green athletes when they perceive negativity and criticism. Coaches can also end up in a confrontation with the Green athlete when they don't allow the athlete to feel some independence or when the athlete is bored because of a lack of intellectual stimulation. Coaches who sprinkle emotional outbursts into practice or contests find conflict with Green athletes who don't appreciate or respect such displays. Green athletes expect so much of themselves, that when they experience their own inability to be successful, their own incompetence, they sometimes react poorly.

Coaches can help Green athletes who are "out of sorts" and frustrated by allowing them to talk about what is going on and by acknowledging their intellectual ability. Helping them to understand the "why," why you have rules, why things need to be done in a particular way, why they must be involved rather than totally independent, will help the Green athletes commit to being part of the program.

When meeting with Green athletes, be very clear and concise. Let them know what behavior is undesirable. Make sure to avoid sarcasm and negative criticism. Make the meeting private so that they do not feel that the rest of the team knows of their problems or perceived incompetence.

Leave Green athletes with a strong, positive message. Focus on their strengths and how they can contribute to the team and the team's goals. Obtain agreement with the Green athletes on how their strengths can contribute to the good of all. Set short-term goals, especially ones which utilize their intellectual abilities. Challenge them to use their intellect to analyze how others have conducted themselves in similar situations. Find quotes or give them an assignment to research how others have coped with similar problems. Make sure they know the coach is available for follow up at a later time.

SOME FINAL THOUGHTS ON GREEN ATHLETES

Coaches may find it helpful when dealing with Green athletes in a one-on-one situation to show them the following charts. This is most effectively done by placing a hand over the second list ("How Others May See Greens"), and asking the Green athletes if the first list describes how they see themselves. The answer will undoubtedly be in the positive. Next, uncover the chart of "How Others May See Greens."

HOW GREENS SEE THEMSELVES:

1. Confident
2. Firm Minded
3. Visionary
4. Under Control
5. Calm
6. Intelligent
7. Independent
8. Perfectionist
9. Creative
10. Determined

HOW OTHERS MAY SEE GREENS:

1. Arrogant
2. Merciless
3. Unrealistic
4. Aloof
5. Unemotional
6. Intellectual Snob
7. Devalue Relationships
8. Critical
9. Eccentric
10. Heartless

Green athletes may be surprised by their reaction to these charts. They think highly of themselves and may feel there is no validity to the second chart, that it is unfair in the way it characterizes them. It provides a great opportunity for discussion about "Brightening Colors" and "Fading a Shade" with these athletes.

Greens will most likely be very uncomfortable thinking that others may see them in such a negative light. Help the Green athletes to understand how they can be more aware of how their characteristics are perceived by others and how they can work to more effectively portray their positive side.

Green athletes may also not care how others think of them. They have a high opinion of their abilities. They may not be bothered by others thinking of them as arrogant. They often think of others as incompetent and boring, so they may not be surprised. Help the Green athlete to understand why "Fading a Shade" on their Green side and "Brightening" one of their other colors could be advantageous. Green athletes want to be leaders, help them to see how this approach will make them more attractive leaders to their teammates.

Green athletes can be a challenge. They portray themselves as knowing a little about everything and can drive others crazy. They can come across as intellectual "know it alls" who frustrate those around them. They can over-analyze things to the point of "paralysis by analysis" and never get anything done. They can portray boredom with everything about a practice, a drill, or a team.

But Green athletes have characteristics that will make a team better. They have very high expectations for themselves and others. They expect competence and success. They are cool, calm, and collected in the face of chaos and controversy. They want to be leaders on their teams.

A coach who learns to harness these abilities will have great success. Imagine having a team that needs no motivation on reaching for goals beyond what is expected. Imagine a team where competence and successful learning of skills and techniques is the standard. Imagine a team that is faced with difficulties, but only looks at them as another hurdle. Imagine a team that has great leadership. Imagine all this and the coach will understand the importance of educating the Green athletes on the team of the importance of being positive, contributing members of the squad.

CHAPTER 8

RELATING TO THE
INTERACTIVE BLUE ATHLETE

CORE NEED & VALUE:

◆ Sense of Relationship

BLUE ATTRIBUTES:

◆ Mediator
◆ Optimistic
◆ Peacemaker
◆ Needs to feel "special"
◆ Cause oriented
◆ Passionate
◆ Caretaker
◆ True romantic ideals
◆ Strong sense of spirituality
◆ Sensitive to the needs of others
◆ Peace, harmony, relationships
◆ Always a kind word for others
◆ Cooperative rather than competitive

Blue athletes have a strong desire to develop a team based on personal relationships, caring, and harmony. Relationship building is a top priority for them and their experience of team. Competition is created by teaching a sense of teamwork through cooperation. Blue athletes want to feel valued for their uniqueness. They are comfortable with emotional expression.

Blue athletes can provide a great challenge for coaches. These athletes are more cooperative than competitive, which many coaches will have difficulty understanding. The Blue athletes also need a great amount of time for developing relationships with those on the team. They will be much more successful if they feel there is a bond between the team members. Coaches who would prefer to spend little or no time doing "touchy-feely" things with their teams may be frustrated by the Blue athletes' great need to spend time talking and working out problems. Coaches may perceive the Blue athletes to be very needy in terms of needing to feel like they are in direct relationship with the coach. These athletes may spend a lot of time asking questions and "hanging around" the coach so they can feel like a part of the program. Coaches need to learn to allow time for developing relationships with these athletes and their teammates. The Blue athletes will be critical to the morale and success of the team, so it is worthwhile to make the time.

The Blue athletes will provide a great sense of loyalty and optimism to your team. They will always have something positive to say to others and will make them feel like they are a special part of the team. Nurture this and it will pay dividends toward a harmonious team.

Coaches are most successful with their Blue athletes when they create an environment of harmony, acceptance and honesty. Blue athletes function best when they feel they are understood, that the coach has empathy for them, and when the coach provides an inspirational model for them.

Blue athletes are personal and authentic. They can edge toward the dramatic sometimes, but look for meaningful and nurturing relationships with coaches and teammates. Friendships are critical to this group. Blue athletes willingly share themselves and provide the sensitivity and compassion necessary to build strong relationships.

Blue athletes find their most joy in team situations that are accepting and where friendships are meaningful and important. Blue athletes' strengths are their ability to communicate effectively, their creativity, their imagination, and their optimism. They always see the "cup as half full" and tend to be accepting and supportive of all on the team. They don't worry too much about the person's "place" or role on the team; they attend to the needs of everyone and provide a positive comment for all.

Blue athletes have difficulty with their team experience when they experience a lack of harmony or caring or when they feel a sense of insincerity around the team. They stress out when there is not adequate time to work on the relational component of their team experience.

PRACTICE ENVIRONMENT

Coaches must be creative and provide an appropriate learning environment for their Blue athletes. The Blue athletes search out interactive, personal, and relaxed situations. Coaches get further with their Blue athletes when they provide process-oriented experiences for them and when the coaches value personal relationships with their athletes.

Blue athletes learn best in group, cooperative activities and drills. If the coaches emphasize growth and cooperation, Blues thrive. They love to work together to accomplish a task or to improve their skills. They also love to share what they have learned with their teammates.

ENHANCING SELF-ESTEEM IN THE BLUE ATHLETE

Blue athletes feel good about their relationships and themselves when they know the coach and the other athletes care about them. Their esteem is enhanced when they are acknowledged for their value and uniqueness as an athlete and a person. They love it when the coach and their teammates tell them that they are important to the team and that their feelings are important as well. They feel good when their teammates and coaches compliment them about their compassion, sensitivity, and creative approaches to playing and relationships. Friendships with other athletes are a source of fulfillment.

Blue athletes have great imaginations and coaches should encourage them to imagine themselves in other roles on the team and to be creative in their skill development. Blue athletes need to be allowed to express themselves, to express their feelings and emotions within the framework of the sport and to initiate involvement with developing a sense of team.

Coaches need to understand that Blue athletes need personal recognition. They respond positively when the coach calls them by name, compliments them, and demonstrates care and concern for them. Blue athletes learn best when they are critiqued sensitively and carefully and when examples used to teach lessons are connected to values.

Coaches can bring out the best in Blue athletes by expressing themselves with an honest, accepting approach. They should be sincere and sensitive and strive for an atmosphere that encourages communication.

MOTIVATING SKILL DEVELOPMENT AND SUCCESS

Blue athletes are motivated when they believe the coach and their teammates care about them. An empathetic, nurturing, and encouraging coach provides the best setting for their talents. Their motivation is heightened when they know that their coach cares about their feelings and treats them like a unique individual. Blue athletes are also motivated when they have the opportunity to motivate and encourage others.

Blue athletes appreciate their coach being available to talk with them when needed. They are grateful when the practice environment is personalized, comfortable, and when there is an opportunity for interaction with teammates.

Blue athletes can especially assist in building team if they are allowed the opportunity. They generally are very good communicators who let their teammates know they are appreciated. Teammates know that the Blue athletes care about them and are concerned about their welfare.

Coaches need to remember to personalize their interaction with Blue athletes, calling them by name and allowing them some "talk time" during practice sessions. Drills and activities broken into parts and performed by small groups seem to be the most effective learning and motivating situations. Blue athletes learn cooperatively and particularly enjoy the opportunity to "share" or to learn from demonstrations by teammates.

Many successful coaches understand that Blue athletes need time before of after practice for team meetings, a time when they can interact with teammates and which doesn't, then, interfere with actual practice times. Some coaches are known to hold short team meetings daily so that the Blue athletes can have some "down time" between the end of the school day, all the relational issues of the day, and practice time. Coaches find the Blue athletes much more able to focus if they have dealt with some of the issues of their day before beginning practice.

GAINING BLUE ATHLETES' COOPERATION

Blue athletes are cooperative when they feel valued and appreciated. A coach who demonstrates care for them and who allows them to express their feelings gives them a desire to conform to the team policies and goals. Knowing that their coach is open, caring, and communicative allows and motivates Blue athletes to cooperate with the coach and the team.

Coaches who demonstrate a sincere caring for their athletes and who are open, personal, and respectful of athlete's feelings will find Blue athletes to be very supportive.

Blue athletes want to know what the expectations are for them, have an opportunity to express their feelings about those expectations, and then they will jump on board and fulfill those expectations. Provide time in your practice schedule for Blues to interact with their teammates. Coaches with large numbers of Blue athletes need to focus on providing positive comments and keeping criticism to a minimum.

Coaches who are able to communicate openly and tell their Blue athletes how much they are appreciated will make inroads with this group. Let Blue athletes know how valuable they are to the team and its success and the Blue athletes will not disappoint in their commitment.

Help Blue athletes set goals by involving them in the process. Know that they could discuss this ad infinitum, so give them enough time for input, and then provide closure. Blue athletes will need help setting short-term goals and being focused on the steps along the way. They tend to see the big picture and to always be optimistic, so they need a gentle dose of reality occasionally, mixed with a pinch of honest care and concern.

TROUBLESHOOTING PROBLEMS WITH THE BLUE ATHLETE

When Blue Athletes act out, it is usually because they feel they are not being appreciated or they have been misunderstood. If they feel their coach or teammates have misunderstood them, they can become quiet, emotional, and sometimes fearful. Blue athletes like to be talked to privately and to be encouraged to express their feelings.

Coaches sometimes struggle with Blue athletes because they need time and the opportunity to reflect on things before moving on. Coaches often don't feel they have that time, so they shortcut the process, usually leaving their Blue athletes dissatisfied.

Recognize the Blue athlete's need to express feelings, to be involved in some team interaction, and to share experiences. Acknowledge publicly the Blue athletes' accomplishments and contributions and the coach will instill pride and loyalty among this group of athletes.

Coaches may find it useful to share experiences with their Blue athletes. Since this group is more cooperative than competitive, coaches who can explain what skills and attributes are necessary for the success of the team and show the Blue athletes how they can grow in those areas, will find willing participants. Expect them to be as competitive and motivated by the sport as everyone else and the coach may set unreachable expectations for these athletes. Blue athletes need to understand how "brightening" their secondary color can really help them as an athlete, but the coach needs to invest the time to help them learn this important lesson.

DISCIPLINING THE BLUE ATHLETE

When Blue athletes are disciplined, they react favorably when it is done privately and they are allowed to express their feelings. Allowing them to explain their problems, and then helping them overcome their dilemma is most favorable.

Blue athletes will feel overwhelmed and stressed when they experience difficulty in relationships at home, in school, or on the team. Those stresses will carry over to practice and disrupt the focus of the athlete.

Blue athletes are often overloaded with tasks and duties. Blue athletes find it difficult to say "No" to anyone. They may be playing a sport, handling all their studies, heading up a community service project, speaking with friends about personal problems, and many other things all at once. If someone else asks them to do an additional thing, they will agree because they don't want to hurt feelings…even if they know they just don't have the time. Better to not sleep at night to get all this done than to hurt a friend. So by the time they arrive at practice, they sometimes feel so overloaded that they can't pay attention to what the coach is asking them to do.

Additionally, Blue athletes may be stressed if they feel their coach doesn't care about their feelings and doesn't acknowledge them.

Coaches can best avoid conflict with Blue athletes by publicly praising and privately criticizing them. Coaches who acknowledge Blue athletes' feelings and who make frequent positive comments will have few discipline problems with these athletes.

When meeting with Blue athletes to discuss problems, coaches should remember the old adage that "a spoonful of sugar helps the medicine go down" and let them know how much the coach cares for them, how the coach knows their behavior is separate from their value as a person and how their positive attributes can help them create a better way of behaving on the team.

Always end meetings with Blue athletes by letting them know that the coach is available anytime for further discussion, by obtaining agreement on how they can best utilize their positive attributes, and by giving them a short term goal. Close the meeting by letting them know how important they are to the coach and reminding them they are good people.

SOME FINAL THOUGHTS ON BLUE ATHLETES

Coaches may find it helpful, when dealing with Blue athletes in a one-on-one situation to show them the following charts. This is most effectively done by placing a hand over the second list ("How Others May See Blues"), and asking the Blue athletes if the first list describes how they see themselves. The answer will undoubtedly be in the positive. Next, uncover the chart of "How Others May See Blues."

HOW BLUES SEE THEMSELVES:

1. Compassionate
2. Trusting
3. Romantic
4. Affectionate
5. Caretaker
6. Nostalgic
7. Sympathetic
8. Sensitive
9. Nurturing
10. Passionate

HOW OTHERS MAY SEE BLUES:

1. Bleeding Heart
2. Naïve
3. Mushy
4. Touchy-feely
5. Smothering
6. Stuck in the past
7. Push-over
8. Emotional
9. Fawning
10. Always a Cause

This may be an eye opener for the athlete. This provides a great opportunity for a discussion about "perception" and how "perception sometimes becomes another's reality."

Ask the Blue athletes if they are comfortable with the description of them in list two. This should provide a great opportunity for coaches and athletes to have a discussion about "where to go from here." Don't be surprised if the second list offends the Blue athletes. They obviously see themselves differently and can't imagine that anyone else sees them in a different light. Help them to "reframe" the words in the second list and see how they can be more positive in their communication of themselves to teammates. Help them to organize their time and their commitments so that they don't overextend themselves, thus stressing out over the lack of time they have to invest in relationships.

Blue athletes are absolutely necessary because they are the ones who are concerned with team unity and cohesion. They are the ones who have a positive word for everyone. They arc the ones who see the cup as half full, who are optimistic about the team's chances this year. They can provide great leadership in developing a successful team attitude, one in which every athlete is willing to sacrifice for the benefit of something larger than themselves, the team. Encourage the Blue athletes to continue their commitment to others, to "brighten" their other colors when in competitive situations, and the coach will have the best of both worlds. The Blue athletes' loyalty and commitment will motivate others to develop stronger relationships as well.

CHAPTER 9

RELATING TO THE
STRUCTURED GOLD ATHLETE

CORE NEED & VALUE:

◆ Sense of Duty and Responsibility

GOLD ATTRIBUTES:

◆ "Be Prepared"
◆ Loves to plan
◆ Detail oriented
◆ Helpful and trustworthy
◆ Values tradition
◆ Service oriented
◆ Conservative and stable
◆ Understands "shoulds" and "should nots"
◆ Strives for a sense of security
◆ Punctual, predictable, precise
◆ Analytical, left brained
◆ Dutiful, loyal, responsible
◆ There is a right way to do everything
◆ Strong in belief in procedures, rules
◆ Values order and the status quo
◆ Comfortable with a formal environment

Gold athletes are extremely organized and structured. They take control of their learning and tend to be consistent in their day-to-day activities. Gold athletes are very committed to their work and take great pride in being well prepared. They prefer practices that are detailed, efficient, and goal oriented. Their focus is on outcome-based instruction.

There is little "gray" in Gold athletes, as they have a strong sense of right and wrong. They value loyalty, honesty, reliability, and fairness. They desire clear, defined instructions and directions and respond to being acknowledged for their efforts. Give them the skills and techniques needed for their role, provide them with the required tools, and it will get done.

The Gold athletes on your team commit strongly to team goals and see the coach as the authority on the team. They will do whatever is asked of them without questioning. Coaches will see these athletes as the "pleasers," the ones who will do whatever is necessary to be helpful. They often are the ones who will voluntarily help clean up after practice, making sure that all the equipment is put away properly. They will most often be perceived by coaches as being "team players" and cooperative participants in the program.

Gold athletes expect their coaches to be organized and to set standards for the squad. They anticipate and appreciate the rules the coach enforces. They enjoy their experience much more when the coach is consistent, organized, and reliable. Gold athletes need to know who is in control and they want that person to be clear on the requirements and expectations for team participation. They expect their coaches to be accurate in the information presented and to demonstrate appreciation for their athletes.

The Gold athletes will demonstrate great loyalty for the program. They will be dependable, counted on to be on time and in the right place, and to put in the necessary time to learn new plays or sets. These athletes expect perfection of themselves and those around them. They need time to acquire skills and would like to perfect one task before moving onto another. They will be honest about their feelings and their relationships.

Fun can sometimes have a different meaning for Golds than some of the other Colors. Joy comes in finding time to be with teammates certainly, but can also be found in the satisfaction found in completing tasks, or drills, or learning new skills. Gold athletes experience "fun" when there is a sense of order in their athletic life and they feel like they belong to something, a team, which is bigger than they.

The special talents and skills demonstrated by Gold athletes include a focus on organization and consistency. Once they commit to the team, a coach can be sure the Gold athletes will honor that commitment with their whole being. Golds use their time and skills well and provide great example of hard work for others on the team. Golds can be a real strong stabilizing factor on the team.

Gold athletes tend to become easily frustrated when they experience a lack of control around their team. They are not fond of change, even positive change, because it disturbs their sense of order, but they will go along with it if the coach asks them to cooperate. Golds don't deal well with ambiguity and inconsistency in their leaders, as they want to know what to expect from them. Because of their strong sense of loyalty, Gold athletes cannot tolerate disloyalty as demonstrated by coaches or teammates.

PRACTICE ENVIRONMENT

The ideal environment for Gold athletes is one where the practice is structured, efficient, and consistent. Gold athletes like to know that Tuesday is the day that a coach runs a particular drill or that Thursday is the day with the emphasis on team activity. They don't really care about which day is which, just that there is a consistent pattern to it. Gold athletes are very cooperative and appreciate practices and drills that stress cooperation among members of the team.

Golds are easily motivated by traditional ideas. They would respond positively to the old slogans, "There's no 'I' in 'Team.'" "The Victory of the WE over the I," or as with the Boy Scouts, "Be Prepared."

Gold athletes prefer a coach who is structured, organized, and efficient. They want their coaches to teach specific drills in a progression so they can learn the whole concept more efficiently. They expect fairness on the part of their coaches. All should be treated equally and all transgressions of the rules should be dealt with in the same manner.

Gold athletes appreciate the opportunity to work independently and to build their skills. They understand and appreciate a system of rewards for particular accomplishments and set goals to meet the expectations of that system. They like traditional skills, drills, and ways of doing things. Golds who experience this type of coaching will strive for excellence and bring stability and an example of hard work to the team.

ENHANCING THE SELF-ESTEEM
OF THE GOLD ATHLETE

Gold athletes' self-esteem is enhanced when their coach empowers them to perform a particular task or role, when they are guided by a clearly defined set of goals and expectations, and when given the authority to lead by example. They feel great when their coach believes in their abilities to perform, gives them the latitude to do it without micro-managing their skills, then recognizes them and the team for a job well done.

Coaches should provide Gold athletes with the opportunity to display leadership; they hunger for this opportunity to be a role model and to be helpful to their teammates. Coaches need to encourage Gold athletes to ask questions. Often, the Gold athletes simply accept what is said by the coach, the authority, and don't question anything.

Coaches can most effectively motivate Gold athletes by providing a structured environment where learning is presented in a logical, chronological, or step-by-step process, thus allowing the athlete to learn a skill, and then move on to the next. Coaches should clearly set goals and rules and guidelines. Golds will cooperate with the coach on these if they clearly understand the direction the coach wants to head. Golds are generally very hard workers; they appreciate it when their coaches acknowledge their work ethic and compliment them on their efforts. Golds will often hang around after practice, not only to help, but also to work on skills they feel they haven't perfected yet. They appreciate the coach who will spend some individual time with them after a practice.

Praise Gold athletes for their accomplishments and contributions to the team. They appreciate it when their coaches notice their efficiency and sense of responsibility. These are the kids who will "run through a wall" for a coach; the coach should be sure not to take them for granted, to let them know the coach notices their commitment.

MOTIVATING SKILL DEVELOPMENT AND SUCCESS

Gold athletes are motivated by coaches who define their expectations, provide the tools and skills needed to achieve them, then allow the Gold athletes some opportunity for leadership. They are encouraged by acknowledgment of their successes along the way, but are ultimately driven by achieving the defined long-term goals.

As noted earlier, coaches need to: demonstrate organization and consistency to really reach the Gold athletes; be clear on the rules and requirements for being a member of the squad; plan practices that are structured, specific, sequential, and clear. Gold athletes respond best in these situations.

When trying to figure out how the Gold athletes can best contribute to the development of the team, coaches will want to assign tasks to the Golds that effectively utilize their characteristics. These athletes are leaders who will model hard work, dependability, commitment, and organization if allowed and encouraged.

Provide Gold athletes with practice situations that allow them to develop teamwork and provide leadership in the process. They appreciate immediate feedback, structured expectations, and drills and activities with specific time limits. Start and end practice on time as they have a strong sense of order and fairness. They have planned their day and their studies around practice time and expect that time will not be encroached upon by the coach.

These athletes can provide a tremendous model of honesty, responsibility, reliability, and organization if given the opportunity and proper acknowledgment for their talents. They want to help the coach and the team to develop into the "best they can be," so provide them with the chance to be a part of the growth in team character and chemistry.

GAINING GOLD ATHLETES' COOPERATION

Coaches will get Gold athletes' total cooperation by leading by example. The coach knows the way, shows the way, and goes the way. If organization, accuracy, consistency, and fairness are the living model, Gold athletes are happy campers. Clearly define expectations and procedures and Gold athletes will meet and adhere to them. Act impulsively and continually alter course, and Gold athletes will struggle.

Coaches have high expectations for themselves and their teams. Gold athletes accept those high expectations so long as the coach is consistent and fair in their application. Coaches should keep their expectations and procedures clear, make specific tasks and responsibilities concrete and explicit, and communicate who is responsible for what and when. Then they will truly be in touch with the Gold athletes.

Coaches need to fight the tendency to change tasks quickly or impulsively when dealing with Golds. The team needs to be under control and task oriented. There should be a system of rewards and schedules and deadlines ought to be maintained. Acknowledge the hard work of Golds and make sure they feel appreciated.

Encourage them by noticing and commenting on their contributions to the team and their effort. Notice their commitment and sincerity. Let them know that coaches appreciate that Gold athletes are reliable and responsible.

Help Gold athletes set goals by having a clear plan. Remember to spend time preparing them for the unexpected, for surprises, because they don't normally handle change, the unexpected well. Make clear to them their role on the team, their responsibilities at their position, and the coach will bring out the best in Golds. Be watchful that Golds aren't too hard on themselves, always expecting perfection, always thinking that people are watching. These athletes may fall into the habit of not trying new things, new skills, new concepts, because of their fear of public failure. Help them by encouraging, communicating, and appreciating them.

TROUBLESHOOTING PROBLEMS
WITH THE GOLD ATHLETE

When Gold athletes have problems with their coach, they want to be dealt with in an honest, direct manner. They want the issues identified and the opportunity to resolve them. If expectations are clearly defined and they feel supported in their development, they will aggressively attack and correct their personal deficiencies. Ambiguity and lack of feeling supported by the coach will only exacerbate the problem.

When it is necessary to change or adjust goals, practices, philosophy in a program, coaches can find ways for the Golds to hang on to a bit of the tradition of the program, explain clearly to them the new structure, new goals established, and acknowledge their role in helping to bring about the necessary changes. This way coaches get the Gold athletes to feel like they are working with the coach to upgrade and further develop the program and the team.

When trouble with Gold athletes occurs, coaches need to ask themselves if they have acknowledged them adequately or if they have simply taken them for granted. Have coaches shared with Golds how they can positively contribute to team development? Have coaches shared their philosophy and the values and goals of the program adequately to get the Gold athlete to work with them? Have coaches used positive reinforcement and encouragement while explaining why it is important to respond positively to team rules and regulations?

Coaches can more effectively communicate with Gold athletes when they understand that these are kids who are committed to the program and the coach's goals, but who need to feel that they are a part of the process. They Gold athlete wants to be a leader, a role model, but has to buy into the program. Communicate openly, efficiently about how the coach sees the Gold athlete as an integral part of the team.

DISCIPLINING GOLD ATHLETES

When disciplined, Gold athletes prefer to have their coach clearly explain the issues precipitating the action and the specific disciplinary sanction. They would like to have a detailed improvement plan and be given the opportunity to correct those areas needing attention. An honest assessment and defined goals, along with their respect for authority, will motivate them to continue to grow as an athlete.

Discipline situations arise for Gold athletes when they feel disorganization in their lives, either because their own commitments are out of control or because their coach has not lived up to their expectation in this area. Gold athletes don't deal well with practices that are disrupted by teammates who don't appear to be focused or committed. Lots of changes in routine or unclear directions for a drill or activity can throw Gold athletes into confusion that could lead to a discipline situation for the coach.

It is most often best to avoid confrontation with Gold athletes by appealing to their sense of right and wrong and by stating expectations clearly and in an uncomplicated manner.

Meetings with Gold athletes should be short and to the point. Present the problem clearly, calmly, and directly. Make sure Gold athletes know that the coach sees them as athletes who really do want to do what is right.

End meetings with Gold athletes by reviewing any agreements made at the meeting regarding how the Gold athletes can be positive, contributing members of the team. Coaches should let the athlete know that they are always available should further questions or problems arise.

SOME FINAL THOUGHTS ON GOLD ATHLETES

Coaches may find it helpful, when dealing with Gold athletes in a one-on-one situation to show them the following charts. This is most effectively done by placing a hand over the second list ("How Others May See Golds"), and asking the Gold athletes if the first list describes how they see themselves. The answer will undoubtedly be in the positive. Next, uncover the chart of "How Others May See Golds."

HOW GOLDS SEE THEMSELVES:

1. Firm
2. Conservative
3. Strong Willed
4. Having a View
5. Orderly
6. Realist
7. Stable
8. Directive
9. Moral Standards
10. Assertive

HOW OTHERS MAY SEE GOLDS:

1. Rigid
2. Boring
3. Stubborn
4. Opinionated
5. System Bound
6. Unimaginative
7. Predictable
8. Bossy
9. Judgmental
10. Controlling

Gold athletes may be surprised by their reaction to these charts. They think highly of themselves and may feel there is no validity to the second chart, that it is unfair in the way it characterizes them. It provides a great opportunity for discussion about "Brightening Colors" and "Fading a Shade" with these athletes.

Golds will most likely be very uncomfortable thinking that others may see them in such a negative light. Help the Gold athletes to understand how they can be more aware of how their characteristics are perceived by others and how they can work to more effectively portray their positive side.

Gold athletes are the most loyal, committed athletes a coach has on a team. They will work hard at practice and in contests. They may have some fear of failure that the coach will have to address, but they will commit themselves fully to the coach and the program if encouraged. The Gold athletes will provide leadership and organization for the team and they will be great role models for hard work and dedication.

Work to make the Gold athletes feel like an integral part of the program and they will reward the coach with their stability, reliability, and loyalty. The have a strong sense of right and wrong and will be a great example for their teammates. Show them appreciation and they will "run through the wall" for their coach and their team.

CHAPTER 10

THERE IS NO SUCH THING AS A "WIN-WIN" SITUATION!

I have always wondered about this statement. I always fretted about this pet peeve of mine in my days as an athletic director. How could anyone not want to find a "win-win" solution to a problem? Everybody wins; how sweet is that?

In the reality of life, if there were a win-win solution, there wouldn't be a problem. By definition, there is a problem because two sides can't agree on how best to proceed. If both sides could get what they wanted, there would be no disagreement, would there?

So how does this phrase get into our nomenclature?

We live in a world today where we want everybody to be happy all the time. Hence we speak of "win-win" situations. Everybody can be happy and win. But is that reality?

Americans too often think in terms of winning and losing. One either wins or loses, right? Yet life and our relationships are a series of complicated dances in which we give up a little of what we want in order to maintain a relationship with another. That is what we start teaching our children from a very early age. They can't always have what they want, when they want it. They must learn to be part of a family and cooperate. We teach children at the earliest of ages about the "victory of the WE over the I".

If by "win-win," one means, "you give up a little of what you want, and I will give up a little of what I want, and we will compromise," then I would understand and agree. But compromise implies a meeting of the minds somewhere in the middle. That means I have to let go of winning, of getting my way, and be satisfied with a partial solution or compromise in order to agree on a solution.

Those who like to use the phrase "win-win" often really mean that they want you to give in so the other side will be happy. I have seen administrators who are trying to keep parents happy by pressuring coaches to let go of one of their rules so that the parent's son or daughter can still participate. "I know you don't let kids miss practice, but this is really an exceptional case, and, by the way, don't penalize the kid by not playing him or her. It can't hurt just this once. It would be a "win-win" for everyone. What do you say?"

We should be trying to find ways to make matters work for the benefit of all. We ought to be teaching and modeling lessons to our athletes about compromising and working together to find solutions. But the sooner we get beyond the misconception that a good compromise is only the one where everyone gets what they want, the better off we will all be. Compromise by definition requires giving up some of what I had hoped to obtain. I sacrifice part of what I want in order to work out an arrangement that will benefit all.

Let's focus on teaching compromise and sacrifice rather than winning and losing. Compromise is a process of eliminating what is less good or downright bad in either position. In other words, it is an intelligent and reasonable discovery of the *common* good. Hence it is not a surrender of personal integrity. Try it! We will all be better for it.

CHAPTER 11

THERE IS NO SUCH THING AS A LEVEL PLAYING FIELD!

We hear all the time about how people are always concerned about creating a "level playing field." Most rules in our state high school handbooks result from the attempt to equal things out. But can it really be done?

Can we provide for equal competition between public and private schools? Between private schools and Catholic schools? Between city and suburban schools? Between large and small schools? Between small schools in agricultural communities and small schools in urban settings?

The real question is, "Do we really need to try to equalize competition?" If that is the real goal, then why do we even need to keep score?

Why do high school sports exist? I have yet to find a school with a mission or vision statement for the school or athletic department that includes goals such as winning a league, district, or state championship, or sending a certain percentage of their athletes to college on athletic scholarships, or obtaining notoriety in the sports sections of the local paper for one of its athletes. So why, when we use the phrase "equal competition," is "equal" the more important part of the phrase than "competition"? Why isn't a "playing field" essential rather than a "level" one?

Don't our programs exist as a philosophical value to teach our athletes about themselves and competition? Don't they exist to teach kids to work harder, to learn to work together, to learn that the team is more important than the individual ("the victory of the We over the I"), and to learn to win and lose with dignity and respect?

Too often, the "level playing field" promotes mediocrity. If we need to level playing fields so everyone has a shot to go to a state tourney, if we add extra state tourneys and let every school play for a mythical championship, then we certainly would have leveled the field. But what would we really have taught our student athletes?

Practically, there are far too many variables in a contest to figure out how to level the field. One team's kids come from an area that emphasizes baseball, another basketball, and another soccer, in their little league and park department programs. In academic reporting, does a 2.0 GPA at one school exactly duplicate what a 2.0 GPA means at another? Do we think it necessary to legislate that all communities, urban, suburban, or rural, large or small, must be the same?

There seems to be little debate about whether there should be restrictions against schools bringing in the best athletes unfairly. We would find near universal agreement to that. There should also be restrictions about age, for instance, because it is a safety issue more than a "level playing field" issue.

But, is it possible to attain a level playing field? NO. Is it desirable to try? Or does it tell some of our kids that they will never be good enough unless we change the rules to benefit them? Is that the message we want to send to our youth?

When we revisit why athletic programs exist in our schools, we find they exist for reasons unrelated to winning and losing—teaching character, integrity, sportsmanship, and the skills of working with others to reach a common goal. Otherwise, why do they continue despite not "winning the championship"? Let's get refocused on why we advocate high school sports and forget about the idea of "level playing fields." Our kids will be better for it!

CHAPTER 12

DOES CHARACTER COUNT?

Successful teams are willing to be held accountable and coaches must care enough to correct and hold players to a proper standard. An open line of communication must exist if teams are going to grow. With this growth comes a sense of responsibility to your team and to the game. Players and coaches need to remember they are not bigger than the game and that the focus of attention should remain with the team and not individuals.

Pat Conroy in his book entitled, *My Losing Season*, talks about his senior year playing basketball at the Citadel. The book points out the several frustrations he had as a young man and his frustration with a head coach who showed little compassion for his players. As often is the case, he eventually realizes the coach was simply pushing his players to reach goals most felt were unattainable and, more importantly, he was preparing his young players for the triumphs and disappointments of the real world. Throughout the story the main element is the character this coach was working to establish in his players and his relentless approach to "doing things right."

In the professional athletic world we view today, sometimes it is really hard to see where character is being taught or displayed. Free agency certainly does not encourage a spirit of "Team" based upon individual statistics and individual incentive clauses built into contracts. Using a sharpie or cell phone to draw attention to yourself is not entertaining, but is a form of drawing attention to yourself or "showboating." How can we teach character and, more importantly, how can we encourage the importance and need for character in our youth when all too often our role models fall short in providing the lessons needed?

The first step in teaching "character" is to encourage players and coaches to understand the need for a positive and productive attitude. If we truly believe we are in charge of our own attitude all the time and we realize the "90-10 rule" (life is 10% of what happens to me and 90% of how I respond to it), then our attitude becomes a compass for our character. Coaches need to establish limits and hold players to them. Being part of a group is vital to all of us. For decades, gangs have grown in different neighborhoods throughout the country as a result of the need to belong. The desire to belong, to be part of a team, is established by the leader or "coach" of any organization. Team members will gravitate to the level of leadership from the top. Some behaviors can become detrimental to the team and have a negative effect upon the group or individual attitudes. Production diminishes and changes are needed.

Dr. John Maxwell, *Maximum Impact* founder and well-known author and speaker, refers to this as "working together precedes winning together." Focusing on your team and not yourself helps establish a sense of self-esteem throughout the team. This helps by creating the "winning attitude" by sharing in the rewards of victory for all and not just what's in it for me. Dr. Nathaniel Branden discusses self-esteem as the key to success or failure. He also says "self-esteem holds the key to understanding ourselves and other people. I cannot think of a single psychological problem that is not traceable to a poor self-concept." Coaches need to nurture their athlete's self-esteem in order to get the most and the best out of them.

Self-esteem is a foundation block to successful organizations. Using the *Action and Communication Guide for Coaches,* leaders can use different strategies for enhancing self-esteem in players or teammates. For example, the Blue athletes feel good about themselves when they know the coach and the other athletes care about them. An understanding of this will help coaches realize that acts of hazing have no place on a team. Acts of initiation, or older players "rites of passage," do nothing to encourage younger players to develop the character that leads to doing the right thing.

Orange athletes may have their self-esteem enhanced when they feel the coach gives them some flexibility in their role on the team. Praise from coaches is a useful tool for all players, but especially valuable for the Orange athlete. Green athletes, when they receive praise, will want specific feedback, not just a general "good job" or "keep up the good work" comment. Remember, Green athletes relate best to factual information and something they can grow from. Coaches should provide specific feedback and not be afraid to let Green players be recognized for their ideas or input. Finally, to enhance the self-esteem of the Gold players, coaches need to set clear goals for the team. The Gold athletes perform best when their coach believes in their abilities to perform, gives them latitude to do their job, and recognizes them and the team for a job well done.

How can coaches build upon the self-concept of all their players and identify areas where all players can succeed? One way is to understand the roles of your players and create limits or guidelines. It's only common sense that kids join a team to play. Everyone wants to be part of the action. Realizing not everyone is going to get that opportunity in a contest in some sports, how can coaches create an environment where kids feel they are a part of the program? The best time to accomplish this is during practice. This is an excellent environment for all players to succeed. Provide situations where every player can demonstrate a level of success. Regardless of the quality of the player, coaches need to be creative enough to enhance the passion the young athletes had when they first began practice. Bruce Brown, a prominent National Association of Intercollegiate Athletics (NAIA) spokesman, suggests that, "75% of all youth sport participants quit by the age of 13." This clearly indicates to us that we need to provide meaningful experiences for all kids, not just the stars, and we need to develop opportunities for success for all kids. As former Washington Interscholastic Activities Association (WIAA) director, Cliff Gillies, used to say, "all kids just want to be special." Coaches and leaders have the responsibility to examine what is needed to make each person feel special.

Coaches have the responsibility to provide learning opportunities for their players on and off the playing field. Role modeling is a huge part in character building. Players look to their coaches for doing the right thing and leading the way. Coaches assume a big responsibility when they decide to lead young people, and this responsibility includes proper behavior on and off the playing field.

This is all part of creating and establishing character on our team.

Here is a simple test Dr. Maxwell uses to help athletes focus on becoming a better teammate. He suggests that athletes ask themselves the following questions:

Do you:

- ◆ Think the team wouldn't be able to get along with you?
- ◆ Secretly believe that recent team successes are really attributable to your personal efforts, not the work of the whole team?
- ◆ Keep score when it comes to the praise and perks handed out to other team members?
- ◆ Have a hard time admitting when you make a mistake? (If you believe you're not making mistakes, you need to check this!)
- ◆ Bring up past wrongs of your teammates?
- ◆ Believe that you are being grossly underpaid or not appreciated enough?

If your athletes answer "yes" to any of the above, they may need to check their attitude and re-evaluate their commitment as a teammate.

Identifying character flaws may be as simple as observing a player in the hall or classroom or watching an employee when not in the office. How do they handle themselves? Michael Josephson, founder of the Institute of Ethics and the program "Character Counts," says, "We should care about the character of the people with whom we choose to associate." He goes on to say, "If we know their character, we can better predict how they will respond to adversity, temptation and success."

Because we all want to win, sometimes we allow character issues to com promise our team values and standards. Sometimes we even do this knowing an athlete is disruptive to the team's chemistry and is constantly a distraction to the team. While there might be success in the short term, in many cases these choices come back to haunt the coach and the team. Pat Summitt, University of Tennessee women's basketball coach, may say it all when she says, "I work incredibly hard to recruit talented people with character. Not just great moves, but great character. Not just great shooters, but a great person. And you have to be selective because when you start out, sometimes I think, you might want to bend a little bit and take a chance. And I don't ever want to lower my standards because of someone's great talent."

Building character may be the biggest challenge great teams and great coaches face. Most coaches want their players to demonstrate good teamwork, self-discipline, responsibility, and a number of the other qualities identified in good teams. One quality that needs to be promoted more is character. Coaches need to encourage it, players need to be held to the standard of expectation, and fans need to be held accountable. As a coach, what are you doing every day in practice to encourage the player's self-esteem, promote a positive team-oriented attitude, and emphasize the importance of character? Provide these opportunities on a daily basis.

CHAPTER 13

SELF-ESTEEM

C oach, I can't do that!" How many times, as a coach, have you heard that statement? It's emphatic, and for some athletes, it's final. They just don't want to try it. Usually, this is the result of a lack of positive self-esteem. The reasons may be many, and the answer to the dilemma is not easy. According to Bruce Brown, a speaker for the National Association of Interscholastic Athletics (NAIA), the problems athletes bring to our programs are not our responsibility, but what they leave our programs with *is* our responsibility. Building positive self-esteem is a long process, which must be accomplished in small steps.

The "Poker Chip Theory," which was coined by Jack Canfield, co-author of *Chicken Soup for the Soul*, states that in a poker game, the player with the most chips is more apt to play his cards than those with fewer chips. If the player loses, he will simply lose a few but has more to lose on the succeeding hands. The same applies to self-esteem. Those athletes with high levels of self-esteem are willing to risk the chance of not being able to perform the athletic technique required, because they are more willing to try it again. They are less worried about what anybody thinks, or how "stupid" it looks, because they are confident they will eventually be able to get the job done. Those athletes with little self-esteem may have a tendency to say " I can't," "I won't," or will just shy away from the task at hand. Coaches would be better served having athletes with the willingness to try it all!

The definition of self esteem is not how I feel, but how I feel about who I am. Do we feel worthy and loved? Do we do things that give us a sense of accomplishment, and do we know those around us love us? Self-esteem encompasses many variables. Dr. Nathaniel Branden, author of the *Six Pillars of Self Esteem* and one of the early pioneers of the self-esteem establishment, says that he cannot think of a single psychological problem that is not traceable to a poor self-concept. He also suggests that positive self-esteem is a cardinal requirement of a fulfilling life. Isn't that what we want as coaches—to give our athletes an experience that will make them physically, emotionally, and intellectually more prepared to face their future?

Many players have been asked by their coaches if, for instance, they would rather run a 10.8 hundred and get third, or run an 11.1 and get first. Or they are asked if they would rather be on the varsity as a backup and probably never play, or play junior varsity and get lots of playing time. As coaches, the answers appear quite obvious. But, all too often, we hear I'd rather get first with an 11.1 or suit up with the varsity and not play. Looking good is the key ingredient to their answers. It's not about fulfillment or accomplishment, but looking good. This is a self-esteem issue that needs to be dealt with. Wanting to look good is not a true accomplishment. It is only temporary and provides nothing in the long run for the athlete. Obviously, with a bit of thought, the track athlete could figure that a 10.8 will get him wins at other venues, and the other athlete, if playing junior varsity, will only become better by playing more. Coaches can make their programs better by observing these thought patterns and dealing with them.

Psychological studies have indicated that people have around 50,000 thoughts a day, and most of them are negative. Our student athletes are constantly bombarded by negative thoughts and actions, and that becomes a challenge for coaches who need to change those thought patterns. Athletes must see themselves succeeding before they can succeed. Visualization is a key element of self-esteem. If your mind's-eye cannot see it happening, it most likely will not happen.

Goals are an important element of building positive self-esteem. Coaches need to give athletes measurable goals they can achieve. This gives the athlete a sense of competence and also the feeling they are achieving and making progress towards being a contributing member of the team. Reaching for the stars so you can have the moon can be a dangerous objective, if the athlete does not understand the whole concept. Small and achievable goals are imperative for our athletes.

It is important for coaches to understand the concept of E + R = O. This is the equation for the occurrence of an **E**vent, the **R**eaction of the observer, and the **O**utcome the two can have on the person and the people around. We have all noticed the reaction of athletes when adverse conditions materialize in a game. For instance in baseball, the shortstop may commit an error and the reaction of the team varies from one player to another. Some may hang their heads and respond negatively to the shortstop, while others may encourage the shortstop to forget it and get ready for the next play. The positive approach of these people will have a more helpful outcome than the negative group.

False Experiences Appearing Real (FEAR) is a major handicap for our athletes. The fear of being ridiculed by peers, the fear of looking bad to the coach, their parents, or their girlfriend or boyfriend. Coaches must convince their athletes that what happens to us is usually not remembered by anyone but us.

SELF ESTEEM AND TRUE COLORS

Blue athletes want coaches who allow them to be able to express themselves and feel like they are making a contribution to the team. When they are not being as competitive as the coach would like them to be, it is essential to give them "team reasons" for competing. When Blues emote, the coach needs to acknowledge their emotions. Blues can be stressed when there is conflict on the team and there is a lack of a team atmosphere. Blues care deeply about harmony, so team conflict is a major stressor to them. Blues can be extremely stressed if they feel rejected by teammates or the coach, there is a lack of cooperation on the team, the coach is too rigid or negative, or they just don't feel like they are appreciated. When any or all of these happen, your Blue athletes will not perform to their potential. Even though our Blue athletes may not be our most competitive team members, they have a calming effect teams can find beneficial over the course of a season.

Linda, who was a primary Blue, was the best athlete on the volleyball team. She had all the physical skills that would allow her to play any position. She could set, play defense, and was definitely the best hitter on the team. Linda, however, just didn't perform during practice or during the game. She frustrated her coach, because when it was time to kill the volleyball, she just would not hit it hard. Finally, her coach asked her why she would not compete. Linda stated she did not want to show the girls up in practice and make them look bad, and during the games, she didn't want to hit it hard because she might hit someone in the face and hurt her opponent. These amount to the fear factor. The coach needs to explain to Linda it's OK, because the girls on her team are only going to get better if she does her best, and during the games, she is unlikely to cause serious or permanent injury to anyone. Another approach is to explain to Linda her teammates are counting on her to do her best for the sake of the team. Remember, team harmony is extremely important to a Blue.

Gold athletes want coaches who are organized, make a practice plan and adhere to that plan. Golds are reliable, thrive on responsibility and take great pleasure in being dependable. They are the athletes who want to hear the step-by-step process that will allow them to achieve the goal! Golds become stressed when players and coaches do not follow through with promises or timelines, when they take on too many responsibilities, when things are not put in their proper place, when expectations are not clear, and when they do not know what their place is on the team. Coaches who do not start on time, are disorganized, or are not consistent in their rules, can find that Golds are not at their best and will act out.

Golds can act out by being rigid, judgmental, complaining and can display a negative attitude. When these characteristics surface it simply means some of the needs of the Gold athletes are not being met. They can be your best team members unless they get overly stressed.

Sean was an exceptional athlete. He was up every morning at 5:00 AM to work out before showering, eating breakfast, studying for a half an hour, and then heading off to school. Before this football season, Sean had always been an outstanding member of the team, but this year proved to be an exception. He was not the leader he had been in the past, and was exhibiting negative behavior people had not seen before. Sean's old football coach had retired last season and there was new coach at the helm. The new coach always had a practice plan, but never followed the plan, and sometimes even changed the whole practice. The new coach always started the practices late and oftentimes practices would go 30 to 40 minutes past the scheduled ending time. Sean decided to quit the team, as the disorganization of the new coach overpowered his desire to stay with his teammates. His coach did not comprehend Sean's Gold need for structure and organization that he could count upon on a regular basis.

Oranges are generally the most confident and competitive athletes on our teams. They want to know what the goals are and they will find a way to get it done. Because they are spontaneous, they have a tendency to disrupt practices by distracting the other team members or they seem to be acting out. Even though timelines are essential in team activities, Oranges have a difficult time with time limitations. Coaches who adhere strictly to time guidelines can often stifle the "fun" that Oranges are seeking. Too much detail, rigid practices and game plans, inactivity or standing in line waiting for their turn, or being forced to stay quiet are just a few stressors for Oranges. Because Oranges most often are our best competitors on any team, it is incumbent upon the coach to learn how to deal with the things that stress this group. They need to understand the coach's way of doing things, but they need to have their needs met at some point.

Brett was the leader on the team and his teammates enjoyed his leadership and fun approach to team activities. Brett was a very talented athlete and was an invaluable asset to the team. Brett was always making clever remarks when the coach would speak, and he also had a habit of not doing things exactly as explained, but was always getting the job done. His coach did not know how to handle Brett, so was constantly reprimanding him in front of the team. To Brett, this was a chance to show everyone else that he wasn't to be verbally outdone by the coach, so he always became defiant. To him it was a competition to see who could win this verbal battle. As the season progressed, Brett continued his behavior and the coach became more emphatic in his verbal warnings, because it was becoming more and more disruptive. The coach gave Brett a final warning, and of course, Brett's behavior occurred again. Because the coach failed to have a closed door meeting with Brett, and used the my way or the highway approach in front of the team, Brett acted out again and the coach told him to turn in his equipment. Brett did this with pleasure, because this particular team make-up did not suit him. The team's best athlete was lost, because a coach did not know how to deal with an Orange athlete.

Green athletes are the team members who analyze a coach's practice and game plans. They value their intellect and they see the big picture. These Green athletes are always looking for different or better way to do things, and will sometimes appear to challenge the coach when they only want to contribute. They are independent and strive for competence in everything they do. At some point, the views of a Green athlete must be addressed, and this is usually best done after a practice. Greens do not like emotional outbursts, so may not respond to the challenge of a verbal assault on their abilities during practice. They are impatient with redundancy, mistakes, incompetence and rules that can block progress. They need time to collect and process information and appreciate your acknowledgement of their recommendations even if you don't adopt them. They like to display their intelligence and solve problems and can grasp complex strategies and games plans and can often act as a coach on the field. Greens can be a great asset to any team, as long as they are given the freedom to exercise their intelligence and are allowed to develop and demonstrate their competence.

Susan was on her school's softball team, but she never enjoyed her participation on the team as a successful starting pitcher. She considered the practices to be too boring, and the game plans to have a lack of insight into the other team's strengths. She was also not happy with the frequent outbursts of the coach during practice and games. Often, Susan would offer suggestions to the coach on how she thought things could be done differently. The coach's common response was to tell Susan to "just do it like I tell you to do it"! As a result, Susan would often complain about the coach or put her teammates and herself down and she was often sarcastic. At times, she simply would withdraw and become aloof. Susan often had greater expectations of herself and would not be satisfied with a performance that simply met her coach's expectations.

Green athletes may need a greater explanation of the coach's vision or plan before you will gain their cooperation. Green athletes need to have their ideas acknowledged by the coach with a "that's a good idea, let's discuss it after practice". Even though the coach hasn't necessarily agreed with the idea, Green athletes feel they have been heard and will have a chance to explain in more detail later. Coaches often may find there is another way to do it!

The stressors mentioned here for the Blue, Gold, Orange, and Green athletes can put the self-esteem of the athletes at temporary risk. It is important to note that one incident does not destroy the esteem of any athlete. A series of stressful moments over lengthy periods of time, however, can have an adverse effect on the esteem of any athlete.

Coaches have the opportunity to work with athletes over a period of one to four years. The cumulative effect of uplifting, positive, self-esteem activities can have a significant impact on an athlete. It is incumbent upon coaches to ensure our athletes leave our programs with a little more confidence for their future endeavors than they brought with them. Coaches are powerful influences in the lives of their athletes. Send them out into the world after your program with an enhanced self-esteem.

CHAPTER 14

ADVICE FOR PARENTS
FROM THEIR ATHLETE

In my last few years as an athletic director, I began asking our athletes about their high school athletic experience. Specifically, I questioned them about the roles of their parents in their athletic experience. One day, I had a brainstorm to get feedback from them in order to share it with their parents. I asked three simple questions. First, "What do your parents do in your athletic experience that embarrasses you?" Secondly, "What are the things that you really appreciate your parents doing in your athletic experience?" Finally, "If you knew I were talking with your parents tonight at a Parent Night, what would you like me to tell them about your athletic experience?"

The responses were fascinating and honest. Most parent groups are shocked and, at the same time, grateful to hear this information. It might be interesting for coaches to ask their own athletes the same questions, compile the answers, and share them with parents. Be careful, of course, to protect the anonymity of specific athletes. They need to know that they are protected if they are to share safely.

Take a look at the following responses. In addition to evaluating the importance of the statement, see if you can identify which Color the parent might be in each case. Multiple answers could be correct. Next, identify several responses for parents with those Colors if you were to discuss this with them after a competition.

THINGS PARENTS DO THAT EMBARRASS THEIR KIDS!

- "Trying to teach me how to do something 'correctly' after a game."
- "Coaching during games even though you aren't the coach."
- "Telling me what I was doing wrong after every game."
- "Being asked to leave a field by an official."
- "Going crazy at the refs—because that is not your job. It is the coach's job to question bad calls."
- "Taunting other players, opponents, refs."
- "Yelling things at coaches and getting involved with something that was between the coach and me and was none of their business."
- "Coming to a game drunk or after drinking."
- "Acting disappointed with what I am doing instead of reassuring me that I will do better next time."
- "Getting a technical foul against our team."
- "Don't say, '(nickname), you really look cute in your uniform, honey'!"

Some of these scenarios are mind-boggling. We all know about parents who come to contests after drinking, but we sometimes forget how humiliating it can be for their son or daughter. The same could be said for parents who are asked to leave the field by an official because they were so out of control.

I have several times, including two times in one night, one at a girls' game, one in a boys' game, seen athletes running down the basketball court, looking into the stands, and either shouting or mouthing the words, "Shut up," to one of their out-of-control parents in the stands.

We all know how difficult it is for a coach to have parents "coaching" their athlete at home to do something differently than the coach is teaching it at practice. For a coach to ask a kid to pass the ball and for the parent to scream "Shoot!" all the time causes conflict in the athlete. For a parent to question the coach's ability at the dinner table puts the athlete in the position of siding with the parent or with the coach. What a difficult position this is for a teenager! Do we really want to do that?

THINGS PARENTS DO THAT THEIR KIDS REALLY APPRECIATE!

- ◆ "Taking time out of your busy schedules to come to games and support what we do."
- ◆ "Bringing snacks after a game."
- ◆ "Supporting the whole team, not just me."
- ◆ "Cheering the team even when losing badly."
- ◆ "Telling us we did a good job."
- ◆ "Being proud of them even when we didn't win."
- ◆ "Being quiet unless cheering with everyone else."
- ◆ "Never yelling at a coach or ref."
- ◆ "Making friends with the other parents."
- ◆ "Telling a 'negative' parent to be quiet—Tootsie Roll Pop!"

We had one girl's basketball parent who will go down in "Awesome Parent History" for coming up with the "Tootsie Roll Pop" routine. She would bring a box of the candies into the gym. I never allowed food in the gym, but made an important exception for this mom. Whenever a parent got too loud or too out of control, whenever they shouted at the officials or at the opponents, this mom would reach into her cache and hand the parent a Tootsie Roll Pop. The first time or two, she had to make the obvious suggestion to the parent to put the Pop into his or her mouth. Within a very short time, parents understood clearly that they were out of line if handed a Tootsie Roll Pop. Before long, parents would catch themselves and suggest out loud that they might be better off calming down before they were handed one. No one ever took offense at being handed one and, before long, our parent crowd became very aware of the impact of their behavior and cheered more and more positively for our team, not against the other team.

We ought to encourage parents to get to know the parents of the other athletes on the team. Kids appreciate that. More importantly, it gives parents the very important knowledge needed to be a responsible parent. If we know the other parents in the stands, we can call them up and ask them if there really is a party at their house this week or if someone is going to be home when the kids visit. It is difficult enough parenting today; we must take advantage of the help we can get by knowing the other parents.

ADVICE FROM THE KIDS TO YOU, THE PARENTS!

- ◆ "Don't get frustrated if we aren't playing well or the team is losing."
- ◆ "Don't become too involved in our sports lives."
- ◆ "Stay in the stands and know your role."
- ◆ "Encourage regardless of performance."
- ◆ "We don't want our parents trying to get the coach to play us. It should be between the player and the coach."
- ◆ "If I don't play, don't be angry at me or the coach."
- ◆ "Tell your kid not to steal."
- ◆ "Relax and let us have fun."
- ◆ "Don't make a scene."
- ◆ "Remember it is OUR team."
- ◆ "It is not a life or death situation; it is just a game."

This is a very powerful set of suggestions. Each of the Colors can take something away from this advice. Kids want parents to treat them with respect. They want the parents to realize that this is the athlete's experience, not the parents'. They want to be loved whether they played well or played poorly. They want to have FUN.

Kids love it when their parents come and watch them play. They also seem to love it when they bring snacks and allow the athlete to enjoy the experience.

Parents ought to have a conversation with their son or daughter to find out exactly why they are playing a sport before they start. During the season, the parents ought to remember that it is the athlete's experience, not theirs. After contests, parents should allow some time to pass before talking with their son or daughter about the contest. Kids need time to unwind, to move past the competition, to evaluate themselves, and to "come down" after the excitement of competition. Give them that time.

CHAPTER 15

HAPPY PARENTS

How can a coach keep the parent of an athlete happy?

1. Play their kid
2. Play their kid all the time
3. Play their kid all the time and WIN

I once heard this saying, that this is the way to keep parents happy with their son or daughter's athletic experience. Of course, we all know this is not possible. In fact, several times over the years, we gave parents at our Annual Basketball Parent Night 3x5 cards and asked to write down how many minutes they thought their son or daughter ought to play per game. Keep in mind that there are 8 minutes in a quarter, 32 minutes in a game, and 160 total minutes for five players on the floor for a regulation game. Then we added up the totals. Inevitably, the number was far greater than the available number of minutes.

What does that tell us?

It tells us that parents sometimes have unrealistic expectations of their child's skills or of the purpose of a high school program. Parents too often think that the lessons of high school athletics can only be taught on the floor, the course, the field, or in the pool during contests—that practice doesn't count for anything. Most athletes, in retrospect, will say, "The Journey is more valuable than the Destination."

It tells coaches there will be conflict; and, in some cases, fear of conflict either chases coaches out of the business or coerces them into keeping fewer players on a team with the hope that the coach could keep this smaller number of kids happy. Coaches have been overheard on many occasions threatening that the next time they coach, it will be in an orphanage!

It tells us kids' ideas have changed as well. It used to be that kids were happy and satisfied just being on a team. I remember one season about 10 years ago, where the team's MVP was a player who rarely got on the floor in a contest. His teammates voted him as MVP because he practiced every day as if that were his game. He made the rest of the team improve because he pushed them so hard day after day. The whole team benefited from his attitude. Today, kids often think that there is no point participating if they are not playing. Who benefits more, the kid who participated and practiced everyday or the one who quit because he didn't want to sit on the bench?

What do we really want our kids to get out of their high school athletic experience? Are we looking for the college scholarship, the recognition, the attention? Or are we trying to learn something about ourselves and our relationships with others? Are we not learning how to compete? How to challenge ourselves to be better, to improve? How to push ourselves when we really don't feel like doing it today? How to give of ourselves so that someone else can benefit? The victory of the "WE" over the "I"?

We should all be thrilled that our kids are participating in high school sports. Period! They are occupying time and staying out of potential trouble. They are a part of something that is much bigger than themselves and potentially very positive. They are making friends, learning about themselves, learning to cooperate with peers, learning to deal with a "boss," both when that boss is positive and when the boss is negative. Lots of life-long lessons are taught every day at practice in all sports. Too often, we are looking at the "end" and miss the journey.

It is the journey that makes participation worthwhile. The journey can be a very difficult one; yet that makes it more honorable and worthwhile. The key word in the saying about "play my kid" is "play." This is supposed to be an adventure, exciting. If you remember watching your young child play, he or she was very, very serious about the actions of the adventure. The child probably came home dirty and sweaty, maybe even sore, but anxiously wanting to share the stories of all the fun and excitement of the day.

Play, being on a team, is hard work. One can either "play at working" or "work at playing." Which would you like your athlete to do? After teaching for

30 years, I saw way too many kids who *play at working*, who don't understand that it takes sweat and tears to be successful. When you *play at working*, you can quit, and move on to something that isn't so much work. I saw too many students who *played at working* on their studies and never did more than was asked and often did less, because it was too hard. I, also, saw many students and athletes who understood that they had to work hard, that play wasn't always fun and games, and that the fun came after the hard work and the results were in.

An understanding of True Colors helps us with this concept. During my college football days, I don't ever remember games as fun. They were hard, painful experiences. The fun resulted from being prepared, from picking myself up when I got knocked down, from playing well, and from the relationships with others on the team. My daughter, a five-time state champion swimmer, understood this. She loved practicing and only tolerated competition. She loved pushing herself to be better and faster and stronger. She loved the friendships with coaches and other swimmers. Competition was a necessary evil to find out how much she had progressed and how much there was yet to do. These were very Gold experiences. Green athletes have fewer problems with this concept because for them, *work is play and play is work*. Everything they do revolves around improving competence, so they find it easy to focus on work and play and to enjoy the experience. Blues have a tendency to find their fun in relationships, so their experience would be defined by the enjoyment they get from being part of a team. They would experience fun so long as their relationships were going well. Oranges find their fun in competition that takes place most often in contests. They can find practices to be tedious unless there is a form of competition introduced into the session. "Colorful" practice plans that keep each color athlete in mind provide the maximum opportunity for growth and fun for all.

We should be honoring those who try, those who strive to be better, to succeed, to win. We need to let go of the personal need to be on the court or playing field during a contest and understand why high school sports exist. Only then will parents, coaches, and athletes be truly happy.

CHAPTER 16

CUTTING ATHLETES FROM YOUR SQUAD

One of the most difficult aspects of coaching is the cutting of athletes from a squad. The primary reason that coaches coach is that they love working with young people. Athletes often feel they have been cut because they think the coach has neither the time nor the desire to work with them. They think that the coach prefers to work with another group of athletes. The coach does not cut for this reason, but kids often think the worst of the coach who cut them. "The coach doesn't like me." "He picked only his favorites." "Only those kids whose parents are pushy or wealthy made the team." "She only likes to work with those who 'kiss up' to her." "I didn't make the team because I didn't participate in off season activities."

Have you ever met a coach who did not have some ego? Coaches want to win, for the sake of the program and the kids in it, but also for themselves. Everybody loves to win. No one goes out of her way to lose. So why would coaches cut an athlete whom they think will actually help the team win? The obvious answer is that coaches don't do that; they select teams that they believe will give them the best opportunity to be successful. They may not always make the perfect selections, but they do their best to put together a team they believe will win and build strong chemistry among the players.

No one likes being cut. The clear message of getting cut is that, "you are not good enough." That is a difficult message for anyone to hear, especially if they have been working and preparing for the tryouts. Getting cut hurts. It hurts because it implies personal failure, not measuring up. It hurts especially for the athlete who wanted just to be part of a team, part of something greater than him or herself.

Add to all this, the difficulty of determining how to tell athletes that they have been cut. Should the coach:

- post a list on the bulletin board for all to see?
- write a letter to each athlete explaining whether the athlete made the squad or not and give them a copy on the day of the cuts?
- invite each individual into the office for a personal conversation?
- call out the names of those who are to stay for practice and dismiss the others?
- post the squad on the school website in the evening of the last day of tryouts so the athlete can read the list of those who made the team at home instead of in front of others?
- take kids aside during practice to tell them they didn't make the squad?

What is the best way?

Most coaches have tried multiple ways to tell athletes they have been cut. None are totally satisfactory. Athletes still have hurt feelings and coaches still feel badly about being the bearer of bad news. It is a painful experience for everyone involved.

How can True Colors help with the difficult matter of the cutting of athletes? It clearly won't make it any easier for the coach or less painful for the athlete, but it may help the athlete understand the decision a little better and help the coach to feel better about how it was communicated. If coaches know each athlete's Colors, they might find it easier to transmit the message to the athlete in a more appropriate and sensitive manner.

An Orange athlete, for instance, will probably demonstrate immediate and apparent anguish over the decision to cut him from the squad. If the coach delivers the message straight up, tells the athlete he appreciated his effort, and gives the athlete suggestions as to how to improve or suggests another team for the athlete to try out for, the athlete may hear the message positively. The orange athlete will presume the coach made a mistake and didn't see how he participated in game-like situations, and may possibly argue or negotiate about how he should have been observed or that he should have just one more chance. But Orange athletes tend to move on quickly to other things. They will be distraught for a while, but will often decide to get involved in something else. Providing various suggestions for what else they might participate in will be especially helpful.

Green athletes will most likely be focused on the intellectual and competency aspects of the tryout. They may point out to the coach the perceived errors of the format of the tryouts, that they weren't given adequate opportunity to express their skill and competency. They may debate with the coach, trying to break down the tryout in such a way as to make the coach take a second look. Green athletes need an intellectual conversation about the fairness of the tryout procedures and the areas where they fell short. They expect perfection and probably already have a pretty good idea of where they fell short. Provide them an out. Help them to see that they measure up to other things very well, this just happens to be an area where they still need some work. Help them to see another way to direct their intellect and their desire to be a leader.

Blue athletes will feel as if they aren't liked or needed. Their desire was to be part of a team, a community, but that community just told them they weren't wanted. Blue athletes will be hurt and need reassurance. They may need an appropriate touch, a pat on the back, a kind word. Quite often, these are the kids that a coach can redirect most easily and effectively to join another team or to encourage their natural instinct "to be for others" by suggesting they look at being a trainer or manager. This provides the opportunity to still feel like an important part of the team. Blues would be attracted to such an opportunity and be successful at it. Be creative with Blue athletes and help them find another way to feel like they are part of something greater than themselves.

Gold athletes will often look at a "cut list" and, if they see their name isn't on the team list, they will simply disappear. They struggle because they know the coach is the one with the duty and right to make the decision. They may disagree strongly, but it is often difficult for them to express this because of their strong sense of authority. These athletes need a conversation with the coach that lays out for them the reasons why they didn't make the team. They will most often accept the coach's reasoning, but may express concern if they have the impression that their opportunity was not as fair as others. These

Gold athletes will often accept the coach's decision even if they disagree. But it is important to provide them an opportunity to express their concerns.

Much can be said for the use of True Colors with parents as well. Parents of those athletes who are cut will sometimes contact the coach in either a positive or negative fashion. Knowing the basics of True Colors will help the coach understand what kind of response is most appropriate for each color.

Remember! Remember! Remember! Parents do what they do, and say what they say, because they love their child. They may not always do or say the appropriate thing at the appropriate time, but they act out of love for their child. They don't want to see their athlete, their son or daughter, hurt. They don't want to sit at the evening dinner table with a sorrowful teenager. You "hurt" their child through the cutting process. They feel the need to defend their child and take away the pain. Don't we all feel that same need?

So, back off, don't overreact, don't make quick decisions on how to deal with parents. Don't make flip remarks out of your own frustration with them. They need to say what they need to say. Take the time to listen and form your comments out of an understanding of their values and their needs, not yours.

Orange parents could be very "hot" and excited, even angry about the coach's decision. The coach should set up an appointment with these parents at a later time rather than dealing with them on the spot. This gives the parent and the coach some time to think about their respective responses. For an Orange in particular, time sometimes softens a dispute because the athlete has already moved on and the next day the parent may not feel as strongly about the need to defend the child. These parents will be a whole lot more upset in the heat of the moment, than they would be a day or two later. Remember, also, that Oranges love to compete. They will try to engage you in a "competition" to demonstrate where your logic, your wisdom, your abilities were not up to the task of measuring their athletic child. Don't go there with them. Don't react angrily to interruptions or clever remarks from an Orange parent. Be direct with them, compliment them on their love and support for their child, listen, acknowledge and recognize some particular talent their child has demonstrated, and keep a sense of humor.

Gold parents may be frustrated by what they perceive to be disorganization, confusion, or misunderstandings about the cutting process. They generally have a respect for authority, but when they feel that authority has been abused, they can be very aggressive in laying out what they perceive to be the weaknesses that led to, in their opinion, an obviously improper decision. Be honest, calm, and direct with gold parents. Focus on the positive strengths of their athlete and help them to see a plan for how their child could improve and have an opportunity in the future. Acknowledging the parent's desire to do the right thing by talking with you will help

Green parents will want to get into an intellectual discussion about what the coach was looking for in the tryout process. Then they will try to demonstrate how their athlete fit the parameters the coach just defined in the previous discussion. In most cases, these parents will not express their concerns in an emotional response. They will coolly and calmly discuss the situation. Only if they feel there is no dialog, no hope, no reasonableness on the coach's part will they "blow." If they get to this point, be careful, listen and don't react. The coach may even want to end the meeting and reschedule it for another time or excuse himself for a few minutes, then return. The Green parent will quickly regain control and be ready to continue. Conflict with Greens often results when they perceive negative criticism. Obviously, cutting their child is seen as negative criticism. Express respect for the abilities of their child. State clearly why you made the decision you made. Avoid sarcasm, labels, and ridicule. Indicate that you will be available at a later date if they wish to talk some more.

Blue parents may be some of the more difficult parents to deal with because they will really come at you from the viewpoint that you have hurt their child and the child may never recover from the devastation of being cut. Schools preach the value of athletics all the time indicating that kids on athletic teams experience fewer problems with alcohol, drugs, and truancy, while maintaining higher grade point averages than the average high school student. They want their child to have the experience of being part of a team, and you have just denied them that opportunity. They may give you all sorts of background information that will further tug at your heart. Keep the conversation positive. Acknowledge their feelings and concerns and, where possible, offer them some alternatives that may help them move toward a positive resolution. Let them know that you are meeting with them because you care. Focus on the strengths of their athlete, helping them to see some possible short-term goals to help them find an appropriate outlet in the school for their child's needs. Directing them to another sport or school activity or offering the opportunity for their child to be involved with the team in some other fashion, such as the team manager or trainer, can often move the Blue parents back into the hope-filled position they prefer.

In the end, remember two critical factors. First, all people want to be heard and, second, they want to be able to have the opportunity to understand why their child did not make the team. It is incumbent upon the coach to take the time to answer their questions and to help them move past this situation. Coaches would prefer to make their cuts, get it over with as quickly as possible, and move on to prepare their teams for competition. Tryout periods are generally very compact because of the need to get the team ready for play.

Remember why you started coaching in the first place. You love kids and want to work with them. Take the extra time necessary to talk with those you cannot keep on your team. It does take more energy, but it will leave you feeling more at peace with your decision and will leave a better taste in the mouth of the community as these athletes and their parents talk about the decisions you made. They are going to talk and may be more likely to do so with respect, precisely because you listened to them and respectfully reached out to them.

Remember, too, that we all have all four colors. This brief essay on athletes and their parents' reaction to being cut is easier "said than done." Athletes and parents will react according to their colors. When we are stressed, we have a tendency to fall back on our primary color. You need to be aware of this in your athletes and their parents, but also in yourself. The best advice is to try to help them to "fade their primary color a shade" and to "brighten" a secondary color that may be more realistic about their son or daughter's athletic talent and skill level. Be aware of your need to do this "fading" and "brightening" as well.

If you are fortunate, your school or local area has a team that is a "no-cut" sport. It makes it much easier for the coaches when they do have to cut, to be able to tell an athlete or parent that there is another wonderful opportunity for them to be a part of a team that will allow their individual gifts to flower. Where this option is available, a lot of pressure is taken off the coaches, the parents, and the athletes.

Remember why you coach. Remember that we want all kids to grow and to have a positive experience of our programs. Even those who are there for only a few days, and who are not quite ready for our teams, deserve to walk away with dignity and respect. Give them that chance.

CHAPTER 17

EVALUATING YOUR PROGRAM

Should coaches evaluate their program or not? In this day and age, there is a simple answer to this question. Absolutely! We live in a time that expects us to set measurable goals and standards, to develop a process for getting there, and to review what was effectively achieved. The days of a coach coming into a season without a definite plan and of parents and athletes not questioning the coaches' methods are long gone.

Coaches represent the most critical factor in the program. They are the motivating force in the athlete's development, the success of the program, and in the overall sportsmanship displayed by the team. Parents entrust their child to coaches, expecting them to improve the whole person, not just the athlete's athletic skills. Coaches are expected to take ownership of their programs and to show the athletes that hard work and patience pays off, that all things are possible when enough people share the dream, and that whether in winning or in losing, one must maintain poise and class.

So why do coaches hesitate to evaluate? Many factors cause concern over this issue. A personal lack of confidence or a fear of failure make up obvious concerns. But a fear of how this information might be used by administrators or parents also contributes to concerns over the process. Society's fixation with winning means that an evaluation in the "C or B range" isn't good enough. Everyone has to have an "A" or they have failed. Attitudes like this mean that an evaluation can't be effectively used to help coaches improve; rather they become measuring sticks for getting rid of coaches. We preach all the time that we "learn from our mistakes," yet we too often crucify those who make mistakes rather than using the experience to help them to become better at what they do.

So, coaches, take charge of the process. Don't let others do it for you. Then you can set the standards of measurement and the process for improvement rather than leaving it in the hands of others.

Should an evaluation be formal or informal? Informal evaluations have the advantage of being completed quickly and providing immediate feedback. The disadvantage of informal evaluations is that they often do not take into consideration all the elements and constituencies that a coach deals with on a daily basis. They provide little or no documentation or evidence of success. And they can be too easily by-passed for other important things. If a coach utilizes an informal process for evaluation, it may or may not get done depending on what other events, crises, or adventures may occur. Orange coaches, in particular, could find themselves skipping this important evaluation because "something else came up."

Formal evaluations provide several important advantages. First of all, coaches would have written feedback, documentation of their season's efforts and successes. This written data is easily remembered, checked and tested, and is usable as factual, historical information or evidence for discussions about the season. Because it is written, it also allows a greater ease of obtaining input from all the constituents in a program. A formal evaluation process requires more time, energy, and effort as well as some additional courage on the part of the coach as some of the feedback may very well be negative. Yet, isn't this how we learn? If the coach controls the evaluation process instead of allowing others to handle it, the coach can use the resulting information in a much more positive manner.

When talking about evaluations, it is always critical to keep in mind the "10-80-10 theory" of evaluative processes. Ten percent of the parents will be thrilled with their athlete's coaches. Their children had a great experience on the team and they couldn't be happier. Ten percent of the athletes are just thrilled to be on the team and be a part of something greater than themselves; this brings them great joy. This 10% of parents will let you know how strongly they feel about your program and how you have positively affected the lives of their children. This is the feedback that will make a coach feel good, but the coach needs to be careful not to let this feedback drive the program because it may be somewhat unrealistic.

Eighty percent of parents and athletes will indicate that they had a good experience in the program. Not everything was perfect, but things generally went well enough that they were satisfied with the experience and liked the coach. You will probably get little feedback from this group because they are satisfied and presume most people feel the same way and that you, as coach, know that. This is the group that you really want information from because they see the positive, yet they might have some constructive suggestions on how things might be better. But they may be the most difficult group to get feedback from. Making it easy to provide such information will encourage this group to respond. Work hard to get this feedback and to pay attention to what this group has to say.

Somewhere around 10% of your parents and athletes will be dissatisfied regardless of what you do. They are those who aren't playing enough, or those you had to discipline or those who just aren't happy, positive people. Since nothing is ever anyone's own fault these days, they need a scapegoat, someone to blame, so it must be the coach's fault. Listen very carefully to the criticisms of this group. As we learned when we talked about perspective and how someone's perspective is often his or her reality (remember counting the number of "F"s?), there may be a kernel of truth in what this group is reporting to coaches in the evaluation process. Listen well; ask yourself whether there is any truth in what is being said. If there is, then use this information to improve your coaching and your relationship skills with your athletes. If not, then let this go. Too many coaches focus on the personal nature of this type of response and react negatively to it rather than treating it as part of the "garbage in, garbage out" theory of learning—if it isn't valid, it is garbage coming in and should be treated as such and be put out; or as another generation put it, it should go in one ear and out the other. This 10% is often the group that causes coaches the most problems and becomes the most vociferous, going to other parents, the press, or the school board to air their gripes. Asking them to evaluate your program demonstrates to all constituencies that you want to improve as a coach and that you are not afraid to hear their opinions. It demonstrates to administrators and boards that you are a "life-long learner" who values input and uses it to improve a program. It can (but doesn't always) disarm a dissatisfied "customer."

Coaches would be well served to listen to the 10% that are happy and the 10% that are upset, consider their input, and move on. Coaches will more effectively improve their programs if they spend time on getting responses from the 80% and learning about their needs and concerns. Formal evaluations allow the coach to demonstrate that there is data to support the fact that the unhappy 10% may not be seeing the entire picture. There is concrete evidence to demonstrate that most kids and parents are satisfied the program is heading in the right direction. This is critically valuable information to have at the coach's fingertips. A formal evaluation provides just such data.

What, then, should coaches be evaluating? Look at the broad picture of the sport you coach and make a list of the areas that you will be rated on by the school, the parents, and the athletes. The list will include such things as:

- How does the coach relate with the players?
- Did skill building take place throughout the season?
- Do the athletes have a better knowledge of the sport by season's end?
- Was good citizenship/sportsmanship demanded of the athletes?
- Did the team learn about setting and achieving goals?
- How effective was the pre-season planning, training?
- How effective were the in-season practice plans of the coach?
- Did the coach adequately provide for emergency and safety procedures?

This list could be much longer and made appropriate to a particular sport as well. But hopefully, you get the point that it is better to have an idea of how others will be looking over your shoulder before, rather than after the season. As the old saying goes, "Keep your friends close; keep your enemies closer." Brighten the Gold in you for this exercise and do a bit of planning.

Before the season, coaches should examine the school and athletic department mission statements. Why do athletic programs exist in your school? Coaches need to know this and know what is expected of them in return. Most school mission statements will make reference to a sports program that brings the community together and contributes to the personal growth, development, and education of the athlete. Most will speak to developing sportsmanship or citizenship, and teaching lessons about life, hard work, self-discipline, and responsibility to others, in addition to physical and emotional advancement. Coaches can search the Internet looking at Mission Statements and find they have a common purpose all over the country. Coaches will be hard pressed to find a Mission Statement that suggests that their programs should win league or state championships or develop talent for college or pro teams. Knowing your school's Mission Statement will help you be prepared to set goals and standards for the year, to evaluate effectively after the season, and to explain to constituents the purpose of the program.

Next, coaches should have their own personal mission statement that includes answers to questions such as:

◆ Why are you coaching?
◆ Why are you coaching this age of athlete rather than another?
◆ What is your personal coaching philosophy?
◆ How will your athletes know your philosophy?
◆ Will you teach character skills as well as athletic skills?
◆ What can I offer the athletes that choose to join my team?

Again, coaches can add to this list, but the key is to have a coaching philosophy that is explicit, not implicit. Coaches need to consciously know, and have the ability to articulate, why they do what they do rather than rely on the old cliché, "it feels right."

Coaches also need to also ask themselves why parents would release their kids to the coaches. What expectations do parents have for you? Should this be expressed somehow in a coach's Philosophy Statement as well? It is always important to remember that parents do what they do because they love their kids. They may not always express themselves appropriately to a coach, but if the coach remembers that what the parent does is usually done out of love, it might be a bit easier to listen and to deal with a parent.

In addition to a Philosophy Statement, coaches should have a written set of goals. They should be measurable and specific. There should be both long-term and short-term goals. Remember that the Oranges out there need those short-term goals to keep them interested and the Golds need the long-term ones to keep them focused. Write down goals—both the personal growth and team growth goals.

How about skills? Do you leave this to chance or do you make it conscious by writing down those skills you need to teach in order to be successful? Coaches need to list the sport specific skills that kids will need to master to be successful as well as how each will be taught, modeled, shaped, and reinforced. Many coaches stop here, but isn't it a coach's duty to also teach life and character skills to their athletes? What life and character skills are important to you and your team? How will you teach and reinforce these values?

One cannot go into a season without spending time preparing and planning for the safety of athletes. Develop a First Aid Emergency Plan either on your own or in conjunction with the school trainer or athletic director. Inspect your playing and practice facilities. Put in requests for any repairs that need to be made to make the site safe and playable. Expect the unexpected and prepare for it.

During the season, the focus changes to implementing all the planning and to tying the practice plans into the goals that have been set. Coaches should have written practice plans. This is more difficult because it takes more time, but it is also more effective in tracking details. For those who don't like this amount of planning (Oranges, maybe?), written plans provide the flexibility to make changes on the run without forgetting anything important. Are your practice plans based on the goals you set? Do they anticipate that kids learn best early and late in practice sessions? Do you begin practice daily with something that draws attention to the fact that kids are moving into something where a different focus is required than they do in the other parts of their day? Be creative, come up with something special that athletes recognize and look forward to at the start of a practice session. At the end, leave kids with a positive memory. Most of us ended practice with sprints or some other equally painful experience of conditioning. Is that the memory you want to leave your kids with each day? Send them home with an experience that is fun or creative, or a team bonding experience so they look forward to coming back the next day. If you are a golfer, isn't it one of those truisms of golf that something good usually happens on the 17th or 18th hole and you forget about the frustration of the first 16 holes and commit to coming back another day? That is what you want to leave your kids with at the end of practice, too.

One other idea to factor into practice plans. What percentage of your sport would you rate as mental? What percentage physical? Are those percentages factored into your practice plan? Yogi Berra, in his own unique way, used to say that, "Baseball is 90% mental. The other half is physical." Another time, he said, "You have to give 100% in the first half of the game. If that isn't enough, in the second half, you have to give what is left." Though his manner of speaking was "unique," there is a certain wisdom between the lines. If so much of the sport is mental, coaches must include teaching this skill, this part of the game in their practice plans, too.

After practice, review the practice plan to determine whether the skill was taught or the goal achieved. Then use this information to plan for the next practice.

A coach needs to talk to every athlete, by name, each workout, and especially after each meet, game or contest. Look them in the eye and compliment them. Make suggestions and/or corrections on technique and effort level. Coaches should also find a way to meet with each of their athletes, hopefully on a regular basis, to get to know them, to understand why they participate, to discuss their role on the team, to determine whether they are enjoying their experience (having fun), and to involve them in setting some of the team goals and team rules. This will encourage the kids to buy into the program plus cultivate a feeling that the coach cares about them and what they think. In addition, coaches need to evaluate whether they are enjoying their own experience coaching and whether they are finding a balance between their personal and professional lives.

When the season concludes, the coach's job is not yet finished. The next step is to do a self-evaluation, reviewing pre-season goals and the written Philosophy Statement. Were goals achieved? Why? Why not? Look over practice plans to determine how much time was spent talking, teaching skills, "doing," and teaching character. Was it enough for achieving the stated goals?

Coaches can ask a whole series of questions to help them understand whether the season was successful:

- What was your starting number of athletes? Ending number?
- Why did an athlete quit my sport?
- Do you have an exit survey?
- What types and number of injuries did we have?
- How was the general health of your team?
- Did your emergency plan work?

- Did you meet your goals?
- Did the kids learn? Have fun? Will they turn out again?
- Were the athletes motivated? Were they stimulated?
- How was the team attitude? Individual athlete attitude?

Good coaches find good mentors. That may be another coach, a friend, or the athletic director. It is always nice to have someone to bounce ideas off and to know someone who will provide input and ideas for development. This mentor will be an invaluable resource as you conclude your evaluation and begin to set goals for the following year.

How does all this evaluation discussion fit with True Colors? While the process sounds pretty Gold, all colors are included in the evaluation process. It goes without saying that each of us has all four colors in our color spectrum, so each of us has a measure of Gold in there somewhere. Golds are clearly going to see the planning as a need in their coaching life and as a motivator for them. But the other colors ought to be involved in evaluation as well.

Greens will want to evaluate and analyze whether their methods have been effective, so they will appreciate a process that leads them to conclusions that will allow them to operate at a higher level.

The Blue coaches will want to know if the kids in their programs are happy and satisfied. An evaluation process such as outlined here will provide that information. Blue coaches will instinctively know whether they have successfully reached the athletes on their team, but concrete evidence of this will help them to devise new ways of reaching their kids and feel confident they have done so.

Orange coaches will often measure themselves against a won/loss record. Too often, that is something over which they have little or no control. Some years coaches have great athletes, some years they don't. So Orange coaches need some other measuring sticks to make sure they are progressing toward making their teams more competitive and that the kids on their teams are having fun and being challenged. They will particularly appreciate the shorter-term goals aspect of the evaluation system as it helps them to get immediate feedback, which further allows them to creatively change direction during the season if needed.

The bottom line is that you are going to be challenged to grow, to become a better coach, or to get out. This way, you can be in control rather than leaving it in the hands of others, or in the hands of chance. It is your choice whether to develop an evaluation process that can benefit you and your program, or not. Choose wisely!

CHAPTER 18

DECEPTION PASS

Deception Pass is a beautiful pass that separates Whidbey Island from Fidalgo Island and the mainland, not too many miles from Anacortes, Washington. The views are spectacular from any of the viewpoints or from the bridge spanning the pass. Tourists can watch the tide in Puget Sound change the narrow pass from a pacific inlet to a raging, dangerous passage. A 976' bridge spans Deception Pass about 180' above the rising tides. Standing on the bridge and looking down at the water below can be a harrowing experience or a thrilling one depending on one's level of acrophobia.

The bridge provides a wonderful example for parents and those who work with our youth. Imagine, if you will, standing on that Deception Pass Bridge. Now imagine that there are no railings or guardrails on that bridge, just a 180' drop to the roiling waters below. Would you walk out onto the bridge? Would you walk briskly over to the edge and peer down? Or would you get within a few feet, then timidly glance toward the edge? Or maybe you would get down on all fours and peek over the side? Or maybe you wouldn't go anywhere near the edge and simply walk (or crawl) back off the bridge following that yellow line striped on the roadway between the lanes?

Now imagine the railings magically reappear. Would you now walk out onto that bridge? Would you walk over to the edge and lean over for a view while holding onto the railing? Might you even step up onto the railing or even sit on it? Would you feel more comfortable about walking over to or near the edge?

My guess is that you have the same feelings as I. When the railing and guardrails are there, I feel safe and can freely walk back and forth and enjoy the beauty of the setting. When those railings aren't there, I can't even enjoy the view because of my concern about getting too close to the dangerous edge. The railings give me the freedom to focus on what is going on around me. The lack of railings forces me to focus on my feet and the distance to the edge. The presence or lack of railings makes all the difference in my ability to be centered outside my own body or within.

Isn't this true of our youth as well? If we provide a life for them free of railings, do we really enhance or diminish their freedom? Our kids need to have adults around them, coaches, teachers, and parents, who provide them with the "railings or guardrails" of life. They need to know their limits. They need us to set guidelines out for them so that they can actually experience more freely the excitement of the world around them.

Coaches and parents are sometimes afraid to put too many restrictions on our kids for fear they might rebel. In fact, we may be causing more harm than good by not providing some limits for them. Kids need to know where the "line" is; they need some "black and white" in their lives when everything seems so "gray" today. Whether it is a limit on what time they have to be home, how much they can drive, what type of movies they are allowed to see, or whom they can go out with, kids need to know what is acceptable in your eyes.

We all can remember our teen years—some of us may even like to forget them. But I remember vividly having to make choices when I was a teen. Want to go out and drink? Want to drive fast? Remember Drive-in Movie Theaters? Sometimes I found it difficult to say "no" when asked if I wanted to do something we knew was unacceptable. My parents had set clear guidelines and I could, at least, say, "I can't do that because my parents told me I couldn't." While not a great answer ("Like I don't want to do it because I don't think it is right."), it was an answer that often got me off the hook.

Today, too many coaches and parents don't give kids an "out" by providing them with guidelines. Then it is much more difficult to say "no" to their peers. When they can't blame their coaches or parents for not being able to do something, they more often than not go along with what the others are doing.

Rules and restrictions are actually freeing because they give you an "out," a fallback if you don't want to do something. In addition, they force our kids to make a choice. They know what is "right" because their coaches and parents have laid it out clearly for them. They might choose not to follow those guidelines, but they know they are making a choice, that they are in control, and are accountable for the consequences. When we don't provide "rules," how can they know what is right or acceptable and what isn't?

My thesis is that kids appreciate "railings" and guardrails. They may not "like" them, they may even say that you are the only one who imposes such rules, but they implicitly understand their necessity and appreciate knowing what you believe to be right and wrong. They may not always follow them, but they want to know what they are.

Don't put your athletes out on that bridge with no railings. It can be a frightful experience. Instead, build up those railings so that they may freely run back and forth and climb the railings and get the best possible views of life. Give them the freedom to explore their world and the railings that provide for their safety while they are searching for their own meaning.

Don't give your kids a "pass" on establishing rules and standards for them by deceiving yourself that this will bring lasting peace in your relationship. That "deception" will not last. Say "no" to a Deception Pass for your athletes!

CHAPTER 19
LESSONS OF THE GENERATIONS

Everyone has stories to tell of how they learned life's lessons. Some lessons come without too much struggle, others with considerable pain and anguish. True Colors provides us with a means of understanding who we are, why we do what we do, and how we can best communicate with the important people in our lives. Parents of athletes have a particularly difficult task because they want the best for their sons and daughters. They want a great athletic experience mixed with a good dose of fun. In addition, they want their children to experience the successes associated with athletic competition.

Over the many years, it is easy to come to a simple, but powerful conclusion. Parents do what they do because they love their children! Everybody must know that, right? Coaches and Athletic Directors have difficulty with this one. Their experience of parents is often clouded by the parent's desire to get more playing time for their own athlete, even if it is at the expense of the team or other players. Often parents accuse the coach of all sorts of terrible things to try to get their way. All this is done, out of love, because the parents want their kids to be happy, to experience no pain. No one wants to sit around the dinner table at night with a teenager who is hurting because of a painful athletic experience, so parents sometimes step into the fray. Coaches need to recognize which color is coming out when dealing with parents so that they know how to most appropriately respond. For example, a Green Coach dealing with a Blue Parent will need to keep in mind the Green tendency to have a lack of tolerance for emotional displays. Awareness of the coach's own Colors and those of the parents can help both sides to successfully find a common ground for doing what is best for the athlete.

Coaches and Athletic Directors also need to be able to communicate effectively with parents, providing useful insight into the triangular relationship between coaches, parents, and athletes.

Parents have a particularly difficult task. No one ever taught us how to be parents. There is no training period (except for the example of our own parents), only on-the-job training. There is no evaluation process as we go. Usually after our children are raised, we realize some of the things we wish we had done differently. To top it all off, our kids keep getting older, bigger, stronger, faster, and smarter, thus forcing us to continually readjust our parental policies and procedures.

So how then do we speak with parents about the delicate subject of their children and the conflicts that naturally arise in athletic participation? True Colors provides wonderful opportunity for insights into this subject. Knowledge of the Colors enables us to communicate effectively with each parent of an athlete in our programs. With that in mind, consider the "Lessons of the Generations" in these examples. You will find many similarities to your own life and can substitute your own experience as well.

A FATHER (GOLD)

Imagine the father who exemplifies what it means to be a Gold. He worked long hours his entire life to provide security for the family. He traveled in the early years as a salesman, often leaving early Monday morning and returning Friday evening. In the later years, he traveled by train into New York City from Connecticut, leaving early in the morning and arriving home in time for a late dinner.

The son played three sports during his high school years and the father made attempts to get to as many contests as possible. Football provided the easiest opportunities to make games as they were played Saturday mornings. The dad volunteered for the Booster Club and ended up working most of the games either selling tickets or concessions.

After graduation from high school the son went off to play college football and his dad attended every game he played over four years. After every game the son played, the dad came up to him, put his arm around his son and told him what a great game he had played, even if this weren't always 100% accurate.

Years later, when the son started coaching himself and raising children, he finally realized what his dad was really saying to him, "You already have a coach who will tell you what you did right and wrong in the game, what you need now is a parent who loves you no matter how you played!"

The **Gold** dad understood what it meant to be a Gold. He understood his place versus the coach's place. He instinctively knew that he should not interfere with the coach/athlete relationship by telling his son what he did right and wrong in the contest and what he should have done differently. Yet as a Gold, he also liked to be in charge. The dad had been the captain of his college hockey team and certainly understood athletic competition, but he also knew and valued tradition, loyalty and fairness. He knew his role and he knew clearly what was not his role. As much as he liked to be in control of things like a "good Gold", he also knew that he needed to be supportive of the role of the coach by staying out of his domain. He demonstrated support to his son by making sure he knew that his father was behind him no matter what.

Golds (like the father) understand that life is not always easy, that, as Vince Lombardi said, "It's not whether you get knocked down, it's whether you get up." Lombardi also has been so often misquoted concerning winning. He never said, "winning is the only thing." What he actually said was the same lesson the dad so often tried to teach, "Winning is not everything—but making the effort to win is." The dad rewarded effort by letting his son know that he was loved no matter how he played and that he had a parent available with whom he could celebrate or find sympathy and love. The Lesson—Be a parent (or guardian), not your child's "after practice coach."

THE SON (GREEN)

The son's kids began playing sports at a very young age. The son (we'll call him Tom) had been coaching for more than a decade when he often found himself coaching or assisting with his kids' sports teams. Both his son and daughter took up swimming competitively, possibly because they knew dad had no knowledge about that sport and they knew he couldn't coach it. The son's own son, we'll call him Kevin, would often ask his dad not to coach his teams because, if there ever came a time when a decision had to be made whether the coach's son or another player would go in the game, he knew his dad would always put the other kid in to avoid the appearance of bias.

By the time he grew to high school age, Kevin decided like most freshman boys that he needed to try out for the football team. Since Tom had played both high school and college football, he thought this was great. Now what Tom seemed to miss was that Kevin, at that time, was one of the three or four smallest kids on the team. He didn't play as often as Tom thought he ought to. When he did, Tom found himself analyzing every aspect of each play. Tom could tell Kevin what happened on every one of the few plays that he played in each game. He could discuss with Kevin why the linebacker in front of him should have made the play that would have prevented him from having to make or miss a tackle. Tom found himself wearing blinders so that Kevin was nearly the only player he saw on the field.

When games were over, Tom would drive Kevin home analyzing the game and trying to figure out what Kevin could have, should have, done differently. (Obviously he had not yet learned the lesson his own father tried to impart!) Tom felt that his coaching and playing background gave him insight far and above what Kevin's freshman high school coaches had and that his son would be thrilled to have dad work with him. They began to have conflict over this, as you might imagine. Soon Tom's son didn't even want to talk about the game anymore. Tom remembered stories of some young athletes who stalled in the locker room after games as long as they could, so that they didn't have to go home to replay the entire game that night with a parent. Then, he understood.

Until that point, Tom felt that he clearly knew more about the game than either Kevin or his coaches did. After all, Tom had played and coached the sport for nearly 20 years, much longer than any of his son's young coaches. Tom knew he could help transform Kevin into a great football player if only he would listen. But that was the key—he didn't want to listen to his father.

Before too long, the fog began to lift from Tom's brain and he got the point. He went to his son and said, "I will no longer make a comment to you about your technique, the coach, or how you played the game, unless you ask me a question. I know that I have some skills and knowledge that would be helpful if you want it, but it is not my place to present it unless asked. From this day forward, I am going to just go and enjoy the opportunity to watch you play a game."

It wasn't often that Kevin ever asked his father anything, but their relationship improved from that day forward. Kevin no longer had to deal with a dad who "knew it all" and made him feel dumb or who implied that his coaches were dumb. He now had a dad who let him play and enjoy the game to the extent he wanted to.

The Lesson—Tom needed to "fade a shade" with his **Green**. He was way too intellectual and theoretical for his 14-year-old son. Tom enjoyed the strategy of the sport and enjoyed the challenge of finding solutions to problems. He expected perfection in himself and those around him, thus giving his son the impression that he could never really measure up to dad's expectations. Tom needed to simply sit back and enjoy watching his son play and not feel the need to be in control, to be the standard setter for his son's activities or, for that matter, his life. Tom needed to let Kevin go, to allow him to play the sport for his reasons, to set his own goals, and to determine his own level of satisfaction with his participation. Tom needed to "release" Kevin. It was his choice to play, his experience to enjoy. Tom had already had his opportunity, now he needed to let his son go, to allow all consequences of his choices, positive and negative, and to enjoy the thrill in his role as a father who watched Kevin grow.

THE SON'S DAUGHTER (ORANGE)

Tom's other child, daughter Colleen, is about as far from an **Orange** as she can get, but her story is a great lesson for the Oranges we know, athletes and their parents, who "live for the moment" and see athletics as their "ticket" in life. Oranges, of course, are master negotiators and natural entertainers who thrive on competition. Many of them are very successful athletes. One of the problems in athletics today is that far too many athletes believe they will one day end up playing professionally, so why worry about academic success? Many Oranges would fit into this category, failing to see the advantage of working hard today so that there is some payoff years down the road when they might graduate from a college or university with a degree.

Colleen competed passionately and successfully at both the high school and collegiate levels. She was a five-time state champion in high school who received a scholarship to swim in college. She worked hard throughout her college years and competed in the Big East Championships and eventually was chosen as one of the captains for her college team. During her senior year, she continued to train and point toward the Big East Championships and a chance to qualify for the NCAA Championship Meet.

Then all perspective on this changed! In February of 1993, Tom sat at his desk in his office when the phone rang. Tom answered. With the first word out of the caller's mouth, his worst nightmare came true. As a parent, do you dread the possibility of that phone call in the middle of the night? Do you lie awake waiting for your children to arrive home after a date or activity? When Tom heard the voice, he instinctively knew that something terrible had happened.

The voice was Colleen's college swim coach. Tom knew this was not a social call. The Coach took a deep breath and told Tom that his daughter had just been diagnosed with lymphoma. Tom thanked the coach and Colleen came on the phone. She was in tears, as you might imagine, having just gotten the word herself. They talked; Tom assured Colleen everything would be all right, that they would do whatever needed to be done to deal with this aggressively. Tom made her laugh and she believed that everything would be OK, just as her dad had always told her. They agreed to speak again that night after the team doctor called with more information. Her swim career ended that very day.

To make a long story short, Tom learned more about cancer, and in particular Hodgkin's Disease, than he ever wanted to know. As a parent of a teenager, he knew what a challenging time of life this was for Colleen anyway. As a parent of a cancer patient, it hit home even more how precious each moment was. Tom knew there were days when his teenagers drove him nuts. They hurt him with their callousness and their desire for independence from him. Looking at his daughter, and wondering how much time he had left with her, made him reevaluate his perception of his kids and his reactions to their "growth pains."

The good news is that today Colleen is healthy, having survived with no recurrence for nearly a decade. She now has children of her own and values all she learned from this experience, though she would never want to try it again.

The Lesson—Two really important lessons came out of this experience. First, Tom (the parent) learned to be more **Orange**. There is something crucial about "appreciating the moment" that he, as a Green/Gold, never understood before this happened. The experience changed his life and caused him to try to savor the opportunities to enjoy people and experiences at the time much more.

Secondly, this experience provided an outstanding example for **Oranges**. While they live for the moment—there is a need to be prepared for the future. Colleen's encounter with cancer effectively ended her competitive career. She needed to be able to fall back on another option in her life. It demonstrated the critical nature of doing some planning for the future, for studying today for a reward that might only come several years down the road, for "brightening" some of their other colors so that they may experience life in some new and exciting ways. Athletics cannot be a "be all and end all." It is fun while it lasts, but it is not going to last forever. What will you do next?

THE SON'S GRANDDAUGHTER (BLUE)

Colleen's third daughter, Grace, was born with a chromosomal abnormality, IDIC 15. This means that she has an extra chromosome, one that is a partial image of the 15th chromosome and that has a mirror image of the part that was incorrectly reproduced. To translate that into terms that are understandable, she has this extra piece of a chromosome that will change the way she learns. Her parents have no idea whether that change will result in mild or severe learning disabilities and the doctors say that only time, and Grace herself, will be able to tell how that will impact her life.

What Colleen does know is that Grace, at age 18 months, is 6-8 months behind in development in most areas. She has to be taught every motion of every skill. She eventually picks up the skills, but mom has to manipulate her hands and knees, for instance, in a crawling motion to show her how it is done. She does not pick these skills up from watching her sisters or from experimenting. Everything must be taught, over and over.

Her parents do not know if Grace will ever be able to run or to kick a ball, whether she will be able to balance a checkbook or live on her own. They just don't know. But they are convinced, as Colleen says, that Grace will be the most loved and the hardest working kid with this diagnosis. If there is a chance for her to live what is traditionally called a normal life, Grace will have every opportunity to do so.

The Lesson—For the **Blues** out there, relationships are critical, in fact they are everything. **Blues** tend to have a strong sense of spirituality, they are passionate and caretakers, sensitive to the needs of others.

As parents, the message is clear. Be thankful if your child has arms, legs, and a brain that function as they were designed. Don't spend quite so much time worrying about whether your son or daughter will get into the right school or play the right position, or get enough playing time. Enjoy the opportunity to watch the miracle they are as they run and jump and swim and play. Focus on what you can control.

THE CONCLUSION

The Lessons of the Generations are clear. For the **Golds**, be your son or daughter's parent (or guardian), not their coach—they already have one of those, but desperately need a parent figure in their lives.

For the **Greens**, let your children go—give them the opportunity to experience athletics without you directing it. You had your chance, now it is theirs. Kahlil Gibran affirms this thought as he writes in a chapter in *The Prophet*:

CHILDREN

And a woman who held a babe against her bosom said,
"Speak to us of Children."
And he said:

> *Your children are not your children.*
> *They are the sons and daughters of Life's longing for itself.*
> *They come through you, but not from you.*
> *You may give them your love, but not your thoughts,*
> *For they have their own thoughts.*
> *You may house their bodies, but not their souls,*
> *For their souls dwell in the house of tomorrow,*
> *Which you cannot visit, not even in your dreams.*
> *You may strive to be like them, but seek not to make them like you.*
> *For life goes not backward nor tarries with yesterday.*
> *You are the bows from which your children as living arrows are*
> *   sent forth.*
> *The Archer sees the mark upon the path of the infinite, and He*
> *   bends you with his might that his arrows may go swift and far.*
> *Let your bending in the Archer's hand be for gladness:*
> *For even as He loves the arrow that flies, so He loves also the bow*
> *   that is stable.*

Orange parents need to help their children understand the while "living for the moment" is an admirable trait, one that brings great joy, it is also critical to plan and prepare for tomorrow. Help your children understand the balance between appreciating the here and now and making sure that they are ready for that day which follows.

Blues need to be reminded that we should be thankful for every moment we have with our children. We should appreciate the miracle that they are. With so many possible genes and chromosomes in our bodies, we should be grateful that everything works in their bodies the way that nature designed them. Instead of worrying about whether your children are the leading scorer or the first or fifteenth off the bench, revel in the mystery of their ability and desire to even be a member of a team.

Parents need desperately to remember that each of us possesses each of the four colors. Each of us can "brighten" or "fade a shade" if we choose to do so. Make the decision to step back, to remember that our perceptions of what our children are experiencing may not be exactly 100% accurate, and to enjoy the very short time span we have to watch our children experience the fun of athletic competition.

We need to "brighten" some colors and "fade a shade" occasionally so that we can develop a climate in our families that supports everyone's positive attitudes and attributes. We are a combination of all four colors. In fact it is our blend of colors that really determines our uniqueness. Our ability to draw on all four colors improves our personal and professional relationships by helping us to gain the knowledge and skills to understand the basic core needs of our self as well as others. It helps us to motivate and empower ourselves and others to use our unique qualities and strengths; it helps us to discover and use our natural talents and abilities; and to assist us in increasing our feelings of self-esteem and self worth.

Parents of athletes need to access all four colors of their spectrum. Only then will they truly enjoy the whole athletic experience in a positive, rewarding way.

CHAPTER 20

LESSONS FOR COACHES

Coaches, too, can learn the "Lessons of the Generations." The **Gold** coach needs to realize that order, organization, and discipline are wonderful things. But if the athlete is reading those characteristics as rigidity, boring, and uncaring, then it will not be a positive experience for anyone in the program. Gold coaches need to be themselves and continue to be demanding, but they need to do it keeping the needs of the other Colors in mind. Challenge the intellect of your athletes, develop strong relationships with them, and make practice fun and changing. This way you will reach all of the kids on your team.

Green coaches can be so intellectual and such perfectionists that they speak over the heads of their athletes and set unreachable standards. Kids will sometimes read those coaches as arrogant and too hard to please and quit working hard for that coach. "Brighten your other colors," let the kids in on the challenge, and let them experience the sport with you.

Orange coaches are charming and bold and energetic. Some of the athletes on your team may see your behavior as flaky, distracted, and obnoxious. Oranges know how to have fun and excitement. They need to brighten their other colors so that they reach those kids who need some structure, some intellectual stimulation, and a relationship. An Orange may not perceive those things to be essential. Some of their athletes' needs may be different and the Orange coach needs to take a step back and take the time to consider the needs of all their athletes.

Blue coaches work so hard at developing relationships and making sure that everyone is happy that they frustrate the kids who see them as "touchy-feely" or pushovers. All kids need to feel important and be in relationship with others, but they also need you to "fade that blue a shade," allowing some of your other Colors to come out so that you can effectively challenge them to become better athletes, a better team. They want you to understand and appreciate them, but they also want to grow and to be challenged.

True Colors helps all of us to be "life-long learners," learners who have a better understanding of the idea that we all learn in different ways and experience life from different perspectives. It helps us to remember that we have all four Colors and that we can understand others if we make the effort. Knowing that about ourselves will enhance the important Triangle in our coaching lives: it will help us to motivate our athletes; to understand and appreciate the difficult role that parents play; and to creatively and effectively be better communicators and teachers of those with whom we work.

True Colors allows us to bring out the best in everyone.

ABOUT THE AUTHOR

Tom Doyle served as a high school Athletic Director and taught History during his 30 year career in education. He coached football, baseball, basketball, and track. He is a past president and treasurer of the Washington state athletic director's association (WSSAAA). In 2001, he was recognized as Washington State's Athletic Director of the Year and is a 2005 inductee into the WSSAAA Hall of Fame. He presently serves as the District 2 Secretary of the Washington Interscholastic Activities Association (WIAA) and is a *True Colors* presenter.

Tom graduated from Colgate University in 1972 where he was a three-year varsity letterman in football and baseball. He earned a Masters degree (MAT) from Colgate in 1976. In 1993, he earned his Certified Athletic Administrator (CAA) credentials.

He taught at Seattle's O'Dea High School for three years before moving to Seattle Prep, a Jesuit High School, for the next 27 years. He held the positions of Department Head of Social Studies, Assistant Principal, and Activities Director. During his tenure as Seattle Prep's Athletic Director, over 75% of the student body participated in an extracurricular sport activity each year.

He currently is the business manager for Personal Perceptions Northwest (PPNW), providing *True Colors* presentations to businesses, schools, and teams throughout the Northwest. He speaks at Sport Parent Nights about the role of parents and sportsmanship, and has authored *The Sport Parent's Manual,* a book on effective coach, athlete, and parent communication. He is a certified instructor for City University where he teaches a course titled, "True

Coaching: Effective Communication with Administrators, Coaches, Parents, and Athletes."

Tom and his wife of 30 years, Marilyn, learned many lessons as parents of two children, Colleen and Kevin, who competed in swimming, cross country, football and basketball. Their son-in-law, Jeff, is a successful high school swim coach. Tom has three granddaughters, Katie, Megan, and Grace.

PERSONAL PERCEPTIONS
NORTHWEST

Personal Perceptions Northwest (PPNW) provides seminars and educational experiences for businesses, schools, teams, and individuals who want to learn to communicate more effectively and efficiently. Using the *True Colors* model, PPNW's experienced presenters provide training and leadership for any organization. PPNW enables you to understand how to motivate and empower all in your organization and teaches you to effectively work with everyone on your team, especially those who are least like you. PPNW's staff boasts more than 125 years in education and athletics and more than a quarter century of accumulated *True Colors* experience. Whether you just want to learn "what makes others tick" or you want to learn how to make your business, school, or athletic team work better together, PPNW can help you to bring out the best in everyone.

ALSO AVAILABLE FROM SAN JUAN PUBLISHING

The Sport Parent's Manual by Tom Doyle
   Practical strategies for parents to meet the challenges of athlete and coach communication.

ORDERING INFORMATION

The Sport Parent's Manual by Tom Doyle $8.95

True Coaching: Effective Communication with Parents and Athletes by Tom Doyle $16.95

Washington State residents include 8.8% sales tax.
Add $3.00 for shipping & handling.
Special school and quantity pricing available upon request.

SAN JUAN PUBLISHING
P.O. Box 923
Woodinville, WA 98072
(425) 485-2813
sanjuanbooks@yahoo.com
www.sanjuanbooks.com